JOY

RECOGNIZING JOY WITHIN EVERY CHAPTER OF LIFE

Missy Brewer Carruth

ISBN 978-1-64559-039-2 (Paperback)
ISBN 978-1-64559-040-8 (Digital)

Covenant Books, Inc.
11661 Hwy 707
Murrells Inlet, SC 29576
www.covenantbooks.com

This book is dedicated to my incredible husband, my three children, my family, and my friends as God has used each one of them to beautifully script such blessings of joy throughout every page of my life.

This book is also dedicated to the memory of my amazing grandmother Toodles Dickerson Gatlin. God used and continues to use her life to pen such everlasting words of joy upon each chapter of my life.

Contents

Preface

A quiet road trip for work was used to flood my soul with the incredible reminder of my Savior's beauty. As I drove, my heart was flooded with immeasurable *joy* that comes only from Him. I'm thankful for the simple beauty of my everyday life and the joy that this life provides.

That joy is found in my husband's smile, my kid's laughter, my mother's voice, my dad's work ethic, my sister's sweet spirit, my brother's heart, my sister-in-law's humor, my grandmother's handwriting, my cousin connections, my Inna's selfless service, my brother-in-law's wit, my friend's text, my church's vision, and my Savior's love.

I was reminded to never take one single gift for granted and recognize the blessing of joy within each gift. Following a post on social media, God began to call me to write. Encouraged by my mother, I began to put words on a page. God poured words out of me and onto the page as I penned an intimate look into my journey of recognizing the joy within each chapter of my life.

Introduction

Joy is mentioned over two hundred times within the NIV translation of the Bible. Discovering our one true source of everlasting joy upon our salvation, it becomes one's choice to realize and recognize the blessing of this joy scripted throughout each chapter of one's life. This book is a personal journey of recognizing that joy within every chapter of my life. In an intimate glimpse within the very pages of each chapter, I share the details of my victorious on-going journey—a journey filled with immeasurable blessings, pages of heartache and pain, chapters of triumph and failure, undeserving grace and mercy, beautiful love and redemption, and a victorious ending of eternal joy.

Chapter 1

RECOGNIZING JOY IN EVERY CHAPTER

Joy is defined by Webster as the emotion evoked by well-being, success or good fortune, or by the prospect of possessing what one desires: delight. But I am discovering that genuine *joy* is intended to be so much more. The source of the most authentic immeasurable *joy* is not found in one's own desire but rather in the desire of our one true King—our Lord and Savior Jesus Christ.

Jesus says, "I have told you this so that my joy may be in you and that your joy may be complete." (John 15:11 New International Version) The desire of our Lord and Savior Jesus Christ is that we each find our joy in Him, and within that discovery is where we shall experience the complete fullness of that immeasurable joy. Real, authentic joy is essentially defined by the choice that lies within each of us and is only as grand as we allow it to become within our individual world, which is guided by His calling upon our life. If the popular phrase that beauty is characterized by the eye of the beholder is true, then *joy* is quite possibly limited by the soul of the beholder. As beautifully scripted by Isaac Watts over three centuries ago, the lyrics below capture this source of *joy*:

> Joy to the world, the Lord is come!
>
> Let earth receive her King
>
> Let every heart prepare Him room,
>
> And Heaven and Nature Sing
>
> And Heaven and Nature Sing
>
> And Heaven, and Heaven, and Nature sing.
>
> Joy to the world, the Savior reigns!
>
> Let men their songs employ;
>
> While fields and floods, rocks, hills and plains
>
> Repeat the sounding joy,
>
> Repeat the sounding joy,
>
> Repeat, Repeat, the sounding joy.
>
> No more let sins and sorrows grow,

Nor thorns infest the ground;

He comes to make His blessings flow

Far as the curse is found,

Far as the curse is found,

Far as, far as, the curse is found.

He rules the world with truth and grace,

And makes the nations prove

The glories of His righteousness,

And wonders of His love,

And wonders of His love,

And wonders, wonders, of His love.

These words were written centuries ago and are sung throughout generations to profess our earthly desire of obtaining heavenly *joy* both on heaven and earth. Yet we limit ourselves in recognizing the manifestations of joy within each and every chapter of our life while here on earth. If we truly allow ourselves to discover the reality of what God intends for us to recognize, our mind stands to be amazed. In the short four decades that I have been blessed here on earth, God has revealed and continues to reveal to me the importance of recognizing each blessing of *joy* within my journey. Instead of just waiting expectantly for my step into the promise of my glorious eternity with Him, I have learned the beauty within the *joy* of what He has called me to do upon this earth. An amazing *joy* that is both overwhelming and undeserving! A *joy* that is ever growing as I learn to recognize the blessing among every chapter of this life. The *joy* found in the happiest and the saddest moments, the busiest and the slowest moments, the stressful and the peaceful moments—the *joy* found in every moment.

It took me quite some time to discover that I was repeatedly missing what He so beautifully had planned and designed within my life as pure *joy*. This recognition began to provide truly what I was discovering to be heaven on earth! I truly believe that He desires for us to live our very best life right here with genuine real *joy* beginning the moment we accept Him as our personal Lord and Savior. He could, if was His intent, rapture each Christian at the moment of our salvation, but He does not. Why?

In Matthew Chapter 28, as the incredible story of Jesus's resurrection is being told, in Verses 18–20 following His resurrection, Jesus gives the *Great Commission* to his disciples stating:

"All authority in heaven and on earth has been given to me. Therefore go and make disciples of all nations, baptizing them in the name of the Father and of the Son and of the Holy Spirit, and teaching them to obey everything I have commanded you. And surely I am with you always, to the very end of the age."

He, clearly, has plans for His children while on this journey toward heaven. We all have been called and instructed to not only live a life full of His abundant joy and undeserving grace but have been charged with the important task of sharing this incredible news throughout our journey toward heaven.

I know within my soul that His desire through the calling on my life is to recognize and experience the blessing of the *joy* that is so intertwined through each fabric of my life as I strive to live a life defined and guided by His glory. A life full of *joy*. One that radiates such blinding beauty! A life with true purpose because with this recognition, it becomes an all-consuming responsibility. As a child of the one true King, the *joy* begins to compound as you embrace the calling upon your life.

God, may my life point others to you. May I live a life that exudes Your love bringing glory to You and abounds in the *joy* that follows! This responsibility creates a consistent prayer within my own life as I cry out to God to continuously strip my selfish pride away.

God, when people look at me, may they never see me but always see You. I have learned that not only within each chapter of my life can I become distracted by my selfish desires, but this dangerous distraction becomes a blockade for others to see Him through me.

Thinking through each important chapter of my life, it overwhelms me with a sense of fear as I recognize the opportunity of impact within each page. The incredible impact that He desires to pour into each turn and the incredible impact that each turn has on others. There are many chapters within my life that each hold distinct and important opportunity. I know that God has placed me within my story for a specific reason, and I am striving to recognize the importance of this calling. I must say as I look at so many wasted pages that I am overcome with disappointment. As God continues to reveal the growing importance that is so beautifully designed with each chapter, I also begin to recognize my ability to miss each and every opportunity within the words. So I am on the quest to recognize each within my story.

As a child, I learned early what it meant to live for the *joy* in Him as I watched daily two parents exude His love and example. As one of thirteen first cousins from my mother's family, I learned of happiness that led to real *joy* from a matriarch that always pointed us to *Him*. As a friend, my heart was taught and continues to learn that real authenticity is priceless and expected within each conversation. As a parent, I am learning that there is no substitute for the *joy* that comes from being present, patient, and positive within my attempt to lead them to grow in Him. As a competitor, my competitive nature was one that drives me to find continued success and one that, through my selfish desire to take shortcuts or my attempts to cut corners, taught me nothing is a substitute for hard work. Within sorrow, I have learned that *joy* lies within the darkness, and it is our choice to let the light break through to shine.

As a working mother, within my career, I have learned and continue to learn that challenges build character and improve our ability to recognize the *joy* that so often can be missed. As a wife, within marriage, I have been taught that my own selfish ideology of expectations produces only fleeting moments of happiness, but seeking to live within His desires for our marriage produces lasting *joy* designed to sustain a lifetime. Searching for my true identity within so many selfish dreams, I have learned that my identity is not found in any title, person, success, or career—but only in Him. And lastly within my most important chapter of my salvation, I have learned that true, genuine *joy* is produced only in a faithful growing relationship with Christ.

As I began to view my walk with Him through this lens, I began to recognize and become overwhelmed by the beautiful, abundant *joy* that was and is consuming every chapter of my life! Oh, my word—it is mind-blowing! The more I open my eyes to the *joy* within my world (that has always been in front of me), the more the blessings of each source begin to invade my being. We are truly called to experience so much more than we could ever imagine when living in accordance to His will. If you look at the entire Chapter 15 of John in the New Living Translation, our Savior is giving us the answer to our quest of living our fullest most joy-filled life—remain in Him! In Verses 9–12, he states:

> "I have loved you even as the Father has loved me. Remain in my love. When you obey me, you remain in my love, just as I obey my Father and remain in his love. I have told you this so that you will be filled with my joy. Yes, your joy will overflow!"

Our own wildest, most imaginative ideology of what one desires as Webster penned in the dictionary only pales in comparison to the unimaginable *joy* that Christ desires for our life. One that is only fulfilled as noted in John Chapter 15 by remaining in Him—Living, breathing, growing, and walking daily with Him as he reveals to you glorious glimpses into this new recognized *joy*. If His desire is for our *joy* to overflow, how are we missing it? Why are we so consumed with things of this world and continue to desire the fleeting happiness that the temporary earthly desires continue to provide?

Well, I think, we too often become consumed with defining *joy* as Webster did—an emotion evoked by the prospect of possessing what one desires. We fail to recognize that our real source of *joy* does not come from our own desires but rather His desires! We are so limited by our own personal desires as they are so often misled by what our culture and society deem as success. Each of us desire success and strive to obtain it within each page of our chapters only to find that earthly desires and success only lead to a temporary happiness—never a genuine lasting *joy*.

We can quickly become satisfied with these fleeting moments of happiness and celebrate within their triumph only to recognize later they are slowly fading, discovering our endless search for much more. Our human sinful nature is never satisfied with the earthly definition of success or joy, and we always thirst for more. With each promotion, career win, elected title, earned degree, or any other achievement that we pursue out of selfish desire, we will eventually become disappointed in the never-filling satisfaction that it produces. We are called to rather seek the desires of His heart through each of these earthly successes, using them to bring glory to Him and point others to the promise of real joy. He desires to fill us to a point of overflowing as we seek the *joy* within His desires for our life. Allowing the Holy Spirit to live through us and guide us within each turn of the page, we will begin to recognize the feeling of contentment and fullness that comes only from Him. If we choose to chase the *joy* that this world provides, we will never reach the goal line as it does not exist. Lasting *joy* comes only from our heavenly Father and is waiting for us to discover and recognize it within each page of our life. In Romans, Paul writes a letter providing great detail on how we are called as Christians to live our best life, a life that is honoring to our heavenly Father. This life is pointing others toward Christ and producing the one true source of *joy* as stated in Romans 15:13, "May the God of hope fill you with all joy and peace as you trust in him, so that you may overflow with hope by the power of the Holy Spirit."

Each chapter of my life is encased by beautiful blessings of *joy*. Some are wrapped so intricately that I often miss the blessing by the disguise of the beautiful wrapping only to recognize it upon looking backward. Sometimes within each chapter, we become distracted by the mere fleeting happiness that is within each moment that we fail to recognize the genuine *joy*. As I look at each chapter of my short and quickly moving forty years, it, at times, can appear to be a book on tape playing in fast forward, highlighting only the quickly fading rays of sunshine. Those rays of sunshine represent great moments of happiness but moments that fade with time. The reality of my life is played at a much slower pace, and it is radiating extreme brightness that is only explained by Him.

This extreme blinding brightness is one that never fades and is now what I recognize within each chapter of my life as *joy*. The *joy* that He desires for my life and the *joy* that I am taking the time to recognize within my many chapters. This *joy* is not always found in the happiest of times within the pages of my chapters but rather found within the real moments inside my world. It is always easier for me to recognize the *joy* within the happiest times of the whirlwind of my life; but God is revealing to me through Him how not to miss the *joy* within the hardest, most difficult moments of my whirlwind life. My Savior has revealed and continues to reveal to me the blessing of the *joy* that lies among each one of these important chapters that make up my life: childhood, family, competition, sorrow, marriage, motherhood, support, calling, identity, and salvation.

As one quickly passes through each of these chapters, it becomes our own choice to recognize the blessing beautifully woven between the lines. Each blessing of joy is scripted within a path He has already planned. Along this journey, it is only within His presence that we discover the fullness of joy referenced in Psalm 16:11:

> "You make known to me the path of life;
> in your presence there is fullness of joy; at
> your right hand are pleasures forevermore."
> (Psalm 16:11 English Standard Version)

Chapter 2

CHILDHOOD

Within the early chapter of my childhood, God began to quickly fill the pages with glimpses of many blessings of real *joy*. Pages full of what most would view as the all-American dream, and as the words were penned, I would quickly confirm that as a reality. Blessed with an incredibly hardworking father and a remarkably dedicated mother, my life was destined for great success. Success defined as a child surrounded by an environment that produced pages that were enveloped with pure love, joy, and guidance directed at Him.

Many nights as a small child, I would beg my parents to let me sleep in their room. My mom would consistently try to reassure me that there was nothing to be afraid of within my room. Most nights she would lay with me in an attempt to ease my fear, but most nights that would end in failure. I would purposely keep my hand on her so I could feel her if she tried to escape once I fell asleep. I remember being absolutely terrified of the darkness; so when the lights were finally flipped off, genuine fear would invade. With that flip, darkness would invade. It was a complete darkness that would begin to suffocate me as it closed in around me. Nestled deep in the woods of South Mississippi, when the lights were flipped off, the complete darkness would invade! No flicker of streetlights because there were none, just complete still darkness surrounded by an array of creepy forest noises. An invasion that would be accompanied with noises from the outside woods that would frighten the bravest of the brave.

And for some unknown reason, they had placed my room facing the woods and right beside the front entrance to our country home. So in my young mind, I had already determined that if some stranger would come upon our house in the night, I would be the first victim they would encounter. Yes, a vivid imagination for a young country girl, but one that was fueled by hooting owls, hundreds of crickets, and screaming—yes screaming—coyotes. Have you ever heard the shrill of a coyote? It sounds as if a grown woman is screaming for her life; and in moments of that shrill, I felt like I could scream for mine. Another compounding factor adding to my fear was the placement of the railroad tracks that ran just through the woods behind my house. The whirling howl from a passing train would add to the nightly noises of terror. And a vision of wandering hobos emerging from the woods off those tracks and stumbling upon my house would swirl within my mind. From as early as I can remember, I was overcome with a fear of the darkness and the noises that accompanied the nightfall. It was really unexplainable, but the fear and anxiety surrounding the dark were real within my young heart.

I had several nights within each month where the fear was alleviated. My father worked as an engineer and would be gone several nights of the month. As we hated for him to leave on days of travel, I secretly was elated every third trip he would take. Within a rotation between three children, every third trip would mean it was my turn to sleep in my parents' room with my mom. I am sure my mother was thankful for the nights of my rotation simply to avoid the night-time drama surrounding the darkness that would invade my pink-striped-wallpapered room. I was safe in her room, and as lights were turned off, the darkness was never thick; and the sounds would always fade. When my father would return, there were also nights of great success within my young battle with the darkness. I would beg often to sleep in my parents' room. Many nights sneaking down the long-dark hallway, I would begin my advance toward their room. Our living room was gigantic with ceilings that climbed twenty feet, and the hallway that led to their bedroom was open to the massive living room full of darkness and noises. A scary obstacle that was worth the risk if I could successfully sleep in their room. I could see the darkness and scary beams within the living room from the moon shining through the massive windows, so I would peek out my door; and I would explode down that hall in full sprint almost sliding on the hardwood as I approached their door. As I would catch my breath, I would slowly open the door in hopes that they were both asleep. Most nights, they would, in fact, be aware of my plan and would just willingly allow me to pile into their bed or in a pallet on the floor. On those nights of success, my tense heart would begin to relax, melting the fear and anxiety away. I would feel safe as I fell asleep knowing both of them were right beside me.

When my many attempts of sneaking into my parents' room had begun to fail, I was forced to discover a new solution to my fear. As a young girl, I had discovered one thing at the moment of nightfall, and that was I did not like to be by myself. So having a younger sister with apparently no fear or worry in the world, I had a plan. Our rooms connected by a Jack-and-Jill bathroom provided an undetected escape to her room once the prayers were prayed, the good nights were said, and the lights were flipped. A quick scurry through the bathroom and I would beg and barter with my little sister to come and sleep with me in my room. In the beginning of this well-thought-out plan, she was willing and actually excited for the fun adventure of our sisterly sleepover. And finally the thickness of the dark and the noises of the night would begin to dissipate. I was learning to relax with the presence of my little sister. So as the words began to fill this chapter of my childhood, I was discovering I wasn't truly afraid of the dark. I just was terrified of being alone in it! Never truly understanding her important role within these pages but willing to play the part, my little sister was becoming my source of strength. As time would pass and we both would get older, my sister began to devise a plan of her own. As I think back to the very first tiptoes through that Jack-and-Jill bathroom, I am flooded with laughter at the embarrassing truth—my fearless sister is five years younger than myself. So yes, within her initial agreement to accompany me as a new roommate, she was merely a toddler! Too young to truly understand her role, she thought her older sister was being kind and allowing her to share her room. So as my courageous tot would get older, it would become more complicated to persuade her through the narrow corridor of our Jack-and-Jill. My fearless sister began to devise her own plan; and yes, I was willing to abide. I began paying my young sister with whatever young children could use as collateral. These nights would begin to build the most amazing friendship that two sisters could dream—one that God would build into a true blessing of *joy* within both our lives.

It truly made no sense why I was so overcome with this fear at such an early age! I had never experienced any tragedy or moment within my childhood to cause this unknown fear, but looking back, I truly can see what this fear taught me within the pages of my early childhood. Early within this chapter of my journey, God was developing a desperate need within me. An innate need was being embedded within my soul for a protector, a comforter, and a friend. Looking at the early words written throughout this chapter, I began to understand the depth of character in which that darkness created within me. Seeking light, protection, and companionship at an early age was the beginning of my journey in recognizing the true *joy* within each of those needs. As I would find success within my parents' room, I knew my father, the protector, was near. And at the moment of his presence, my fears would escape. I had discovered the power of companionship and a friend as my young sister's presence within my room would drive my fear away. And on the nights of rotation while my father was out-of-town, my turn with my mother would create a comfort that would melt away the darkness and silence the noise. Soon within the chapter of my early childhood, my true source of companionship, my friend, my protector, and my comforter would begin to fill the need within my soul that would melt away any future fear or darkness that my chapters may produce.

This early chapter within my life would produce not only the recognition of the need within my soul, but it would also provide the most incredible example of a life living within the full recognition of that *joy*. My father, the protector of our house, and my mother, the comforter of our journey, had an incredible ability to cause all fears to dissolve, and it ultimately filled my pages with such words of beautiful, incredible *joy*. Their mission was evident in every aspect of their life. That mission guided by our Savior—was love. God would and continues to use them to fill endless pages of each chapter within my life with words enveloped by love and happiness.

My parents were always planning exciting adventures upon our hill in small town, Mississippi. One day we jumped into our car with my mom for another adventure as we drove around the corner of our country road. Pulling up to the railroad crossing, we parked the car on the side of the grass and dirt leading up to the tracks. My brother, sister, and I jumped out of the car as fast as we could! All alone on those tracks with our mom watching our every move, we danced with excitement.

We all were filled with such anticipation! My mom, trying to calm us down and keep us back from the tracks, would tell us any minute; and she was right. Suddenly with the howl of the train and the shrill of the whistle, we saw the engine coming around the corner. As the train slowed while passing, we jumped and screamed as if it was the Macy's Day parade! When the engine passed at a slower pace than normal, our dad, the engineer, began to throw candy and treats out the engine window as he pulled that horn with pure joy! That same whirling howl that would terrify me within the darkness was an incredible source of elation that day as our dad would parade through the railroad crossing on our country road!

We three would all scurry picking up each piece of candy and treat as we laughed and played upon the rock bank of the tracks. Oh, the joy and happiness that abounded along those tracks as that same laughter and joy would echo through the halls of our home my entire childhood. The engineer of fun within our world was not alone in his ability to orchestrate such an environment of love and happiness. He had the most incredible grand marshal by his side, tending to every-minute detail of our ever-changing life. She was constantly ensuring that each turn within the route of our journey would always be directed to our ultimate source of *joy*. Longing for the day each of us would fully recognize that *joy* within our own life, she prayed over us directing us to cling tight to the truth within that *joy* and prepared us for the most amazing ride that one lifetime could entail. We would grow to recognize that this engineer and his grand marshal were throwing much more than candy and treats our way. They were filling much more than our brown paper bags. They were filling our souls with an example of an unmatched source of love. A love that leads to our ultimate source of *joy*. A love that always pointed me and my family to Christ. One that infiltrated and filled the early desperate need of my longing-childhood heart and one that led me to my Savior.

Zach Williams so adequately describes it within his song "Fear is a Liar!" The lyrics talk about how fear can take your breath away and literally stop you in your steps. It also exclaims that if you allow it, fear can rob you of your rest and begin to steal your happiness! It is truly a liar! As fear attempted to shadow many aspects of my childhood journey, my parents

were always quick to redirect and point me toward the light!
The light in which David so beautifully proclaimed in the first
five verses of Psalm 27:

"The Lord is my light and my salvation—

whom shall I fear?

The Lord is the stronghold of my life—

of whom shall I be afraid?

When the wicked advance against me

to devour me,

it is my enemies and my foes

who will stumble and fall.

Though an army besiege me,

my heart will not fear;

though war break out against me,

even then I will be confident.

One thing I ask from the Lord,

This only do I seek:

That I may dwell in the house of the Lord

all the days of my life,

to gaze on the beauty of the Lord.

and to seek him in his temple.

For in the day of trouble

he will keep me safe in his dwelling;

he will hide me in his shelter of his sacred tent

and set me high upon a rock."

I realize and recognize looking back over the early pages scripted throughout my journey that God would use my parents to pen such incredible *joy* found inside the blessing of my childhood. I would only later recognize that realization and understand the direction of how that blessing directed my life more toward Him. And early within this chapter of childhood, I would recognize and grab hold of that realization finding my true source of *joy* in the ever-present fear destroyer—my Savior, Jesus Christ. I would not understand the impact in which that realization would provide until much deeper within the turns of my pages, but as David so richly professed: the Lord would indeed become the stronghold of my life throughout each turn of the page.

Chapter 3

FAMILY

Living in the country of small-town Mississippi, the outdoors was my playground. The pages of my childhood may have been shadowed with the fear of the darkness at nightfall, but with the dawn of each morning, there was a new adventure to be written. Many of those adventures were scripted by a marvelous grandmother who lived next door.

As a true treasure within the pages of my journey, she sculpted such lasting impact among each page. She lived a life that radiated His beauty through everything she did and every life she touched. I would grow to recognize her as such a genuine blessing of joy as God used her life to write such pages of love throughout my entire families' journey. As the matriarch of such a large family, she led us all with her laughter, her stories, and her love. Being one of thirteen first cousins, our crew had somewhat of an interesting bond. As summer would begin, my cousins and I would embark on days full of exploration and adventure. It was an unexplainable connection between the large group, but one that would lend to pages of immeasurable fun and adventure. The exact details of every adventure upon our hill are shaded within my memory, but the impact of most are sketched within my heart.

"Do you know how to drive this, Tammy?" my dad asked my visiting cousin from Alabama. "Sure I do!" she said with confidence. Tammy was an older cousin from Alabama that was, in many senses, always leading the sometimes outlandish adventure upon our hill. Being from Alabama, she was not exposed to the everyday adventures of my brother and other cousins who lived around the corner. From the time I can remember, this group of cousins, along with my brother and sister, would roam the country roads of this small town. We were a tight-knit group, lacking not in toughness nor the ability to discover real fun.

Tammy was never going to admit to not being able to do something that we all could do with ease. So with that, she jumped onto the back of our small junior dirt bike placing the helmet on tight. Her long thick and curly brown hair was sticking out the back of her helmet. She was ready or at least she looked like she was ready for her ride. Behind our house was an open pasture leading up to our barn with a large gravel pit beside it. We spent many days building forts and racing bikes within the woods behind this gravel pit, but this day we would find ourselves racing for a rescue and not a fort win. With one turn of her wrist, she was off! She took off at such speed and showed no sign of slowing down. We began to yell for her to simply let go; but in what appeared to be pure panic, she was frozen in a full-speed pursuit toward the cliff of the gravel pit. As I began to sprint with the others, it was becoming quite evident that my older cousin had indeed been mistaken on her ability to handle the small dirt bike! She did not know how to drive this dirt bike; and in that passing moment, I began to laugh amid the terror. I was not sure if I should scream or cry as she was quickly approaching the cliff but found myself in a state of hysteria. Within the quickly moving moments, I noticed that my uncontrollable laughter would soon turn to a panic of my own.

As a young girl, I sprinted with my other cousins scream-ing for Tammy to simply let go! *Oh my goodness*, I thought to myself, *she is going to fly right off the top of the gravel pit*. All I could see was the dust from her tires and her long curls fly-ing through the weeds of the pasture. While we are all yelling "Tammy, let go!" I notice my dad in full sprint as he was yelling for her to hold on tight.

"What is he doing?" I thought racing through the pasture. "Why is he telling her to hold on as we were all begging for her to let go!" He was closing in on her as she hit the gravel portion of the pit right before the drop-off. He hurled a small bucket hitting the front tire of that small dirt bike, sending Tammy and the bike flying across the gravel. Wide-eyed and out of breath, I finally reached the crashed bike and Tammy lying on the gravel just at the top of the cliff. As I watch my dad tend to her, I was trying to process what had just happened. Realizing the reason for my dad's heroic hurl of the bucket, I began to realize the severity of the accident. I looked down at Tammy covered in dirt and some scrapes and bruises from the crash. I began to notice something else was really wrong. Where was her hair?

Her beautiful long curly brown hair was missing within the helmet. The hysterical laughter ensued again, but this time, it was uncontrollable! Apparently, she had ridden right through several cocklebur plants causing her hair to be tightly entangled with hundreds of cockleburs. It was so tight that it appeared she had curlers and pins wrapping her hair against her head. We all crowded around her as my dad scooped her up in his arms and proceeded to run back toward my grandmother's house. He, apparently, was concerned with her injuries; but my cousins and I were still very concerned with her hair.

Walking into my grandmother's house, three sisters (my two aunts and my mom) sat visiting in the kitchen. With our entrance, the chaos ensued. Each would surround Tammy tending to her scrapes and wiping the dirt and tears from her eyes. As we attempted to all tell the story of what had happened in the field and the heroic effort of my dad, I could not shake the obvious and hysterical concern for her hair. For hours, the three sisters would pick cockleburs from her head. The pain of that detangle was far greater than the scrapes and bruises of the day. But the pain of our poor cousin was not nearly as great as the laughter of the cousins and our grandma as we watched from within the living room. A laughter that would echo the pages of my entire childhood placed within what would often feel like a leave-it-to-beaver episode. The cousins within my story would create such innocent-and-joy-filled days of adventure. The adventures that we encountered would rival those of even the *Goonies*. Living next to the railroad track, river, and woods would give us a daily playground limited only by our imagination. We built forts along the railroad track preparing for hobo attacks, constructed teepees within the fields in our imaginative tribe village, and we would escape into a whole new world within the hallways of an old abandoned school. As I think back over the bliss of each day of new exploration, I am reminded by how the simplest of joys often create the most lasting impression. My children are often bound by such demands too early within their pages—pages filled with travel ball, expectations, and pressure. Reminded by the simplicity of my long summer days on top of our hill in Johnston Station, I long for a simpler time of laughter and exploration.

Sometimes this society seems to search for the grandiose of life to provide the happiness within each moment. Most are striving to keep up with the Jones's never finding ultimate joy in their endless quest for more. On the top of our hill of childhood, we never seemed to try and keep up with anyone, distracted by the noise of the simple adventures of fun. Looking back upon this chapter, I am reminded of one of the most precious blessings of joy within my life—family.

God designed each family with such beauty, sculpting each member with distinct purpose. Our culture today seems to dismiss the importance of this irreplaceable joy as we deem the joy in things of this world. The things of this world will fade and are temporary, but the love of a God-honoring family is forever. As I think of the laughter and fun of my childhood adventures with my cousins, I am flooded with the impact of each one within my life. I recognize within the friendship and example of their life that God was and continues to be intentional as He scripts each page of our chapters of life.

I am often heartbroken as I witness within this world that families are exploding within themselves. Often, over insignificant issues of selfishness and disagreement, one will turn their back on a family member. I can only imagine the pain that this causes our heavenly Father as He has so perfectly sculpted us for each other. I fully recognize within these pages that there will be times of difficulty and even pain; but just as my aunts and my mother patiently picked the cockleburs out of Tammy's hair, the pain of any detangle is defeated by the patience and love of each family member. This detangle is often not without tears and pain but worth the time and effort to repair. Realizing that each of us is imperfect, I recognize that a family is only realized as a beautiful blessing when led by our heavenly Father. A family living with an earthly purpose finding gratification with what the world defines as success will only fail at an attempt of realizing the true blessing of joy within the design. A design in which my grandmother left as a legacy, a legacy of finding and holding on to the one true joy-providing source of our heavenly Father. A design beautifully etched across the hearts of each of her thirteen grandchildren. Her life lived with a purpose driven by her love for our Savior and her family. She never seemed distracted by what the outside world even taunted. She was so consumed with the laughter and the joy within the blessing of her family.

After having kids, my husband and I made the decision to move back home to small-town Mississippi. The same small town that both of us spent our childhood. Many would often ask, "Why would you move to small-town Mississippi?"

Our answer is quite simple, "Why would we not!"

We longed for our children to experience the immeasurable joy that we had recognized within the blessing of being surrounded by family. God had so richly blessed us both with a childhood full of joy. And as adults, we had recognized the blessing and source of that joy was our family. Family is not chosen. It is gifted and intentional. Attempting to never take this gift for granted, we have chosen to surround ourselves with this blessing. Adding to the pages of our childhood laughter, we are now watching our own children fill the pages of their childhood with a similar sound. Their pages being scripted full of laughter from their own cousin connections, love from their grandparents, and the simple joys of cherishing their family.

Chapter 4

COMPETITION

As the pages of my childhood flipped, I would quickly realize a common theme scripted across each chapter. Pages shadowed by fear within the dark and adventurous exploration with cousins, but all were covered with a confidence produced through competition. A discovery stretching from the dirt of backyard basketball to the clay of national championships. I had been born with an innate drive to win. An early recognition that I would find within the pages of my childhood and apparently would discover within the very similarly scripted pages of my own children.

As we walked into the entrance of the ballpark, it must have been at least 100 degrees. Steam rose from the turf fields, and the air felt like we were walking through a sauna. "I don't feel too good," she said as we walked through the entrance of field one.

"What's wrong?" I asked, looking down at her as she wiped the sweat from her intensely focused brow. No response from number 18, but she was gagging as she walked. She picked up her speed as she headed straight toward the bathroom. I grabbed her hand and picked up my speed alongside of her but would be too late. She had just vomited all over the sidewalk in between two playing fields, jammed full of spectators in midstride. We did not even checkup while proceeding quickly to the restrooms. Her bright eyes were intense as we wiped her face.

"Carlyle, are you okay?" I asked.

"Yes, ma'am. I am fine!" she said as she hurried out to get ready for her game. I followed after her and sat beside her as she prepared for the next game of the 8U Mississippi State Tournament.

"Look at me, C. You do not have to play if you feel bad!" I said as I peered in her big blue intensely focused eight-year-old eyes. She did not have to say a word because in her eyes, I recognized a very familiar drive. And in that moment, I understood the source of her sickness.

Oh my goodness! This baby girl was a competitor, and I understood all too well the stomach pain associated with the fear of not achieving perfection and a win with every beginning of a competition. Have you ever heard the saying she was born for this? Well, it appeared that she had inherited the all-too-familiar drive to compete! As early as I can remember, the thrill of competition drove me. I was unsure the details of this inner drive to succeed, but I would soon discover the way God would use this within me to recognize the *joy* it would produce.

*****

The gun sounded, and I dove as precise as my eight-year-old body knew how to dive. *I could do this*, I thought as I kicked and pulled as strongly and quickly as I could. I could hear the roar of the crowd on the sides and the ends of the pool, but I saw nothing but the black strip of paint guiding me to the first flip of my fifty meters freestyle. I was moving and had no plans of slowing down. With the turn, my lungs began to burn; but I could hear my coach's voice in my mind, "Each breath slows you down. Push yourself!"

And as I stretched to reach the finish wall, I could hear the slap of my coach's clipboard! With the touch of the wall, I swirled my head to see I had done it! I had clenched the win with an all-time record, and wait a minute, I had done it with no breath! My small hands slapped the water with excitement.

As I turned, my coach had slammed her clipboard breaking into pieces as she screamed to the older teammates "She has just swum the fifty with no breath!" She turned to pull me out of the water and still very loud in my face, she proceeded to scream "You just swam the fifty with no breath," and I simply replied, "You said each breath would slow me down."

*****

As a young child, my first experience with intense competition came in the form of the swim team. Even as a young child, my desire to win was so intense that prior to every race and competition, I would physically become sick. It was something that my coach and teammates would become accustomed to; but I never would be able to control. "This could not be healthy for a child to be this competitive," they would say. But I was born with an inner desire not to compete but to win. Even the thought of the possibility of defeat would make my stomach turn. At the age of eight, I had recognized the *joy* in winning; but it would take me years to discover the blessing within the *joy* of competition.

A couple of years later, our community pool would close forcing an end to our small-town swim team. This swim team had become family, forging friendships among a group of young kids and families centered on the quest of competition. Saddened by the end to what had been my first taste of the thrill of competition, my parents were faced with a decision— drive seventy miles north to train in Jackson, Mississippi, or explore other opportunities in sport. I had been playing small-town soccer and softball. But at the age of ten, I was driven by a greater need to compete on a more intense level. I was searching for a more intense level of competition. A friend from the swim team suggested my parents allow me to try tennis—a decision that would reshape my future.

Tennis became a new and exciting passion of mine, providing a new avenue of intensely driven competition. This sport was designed with the fiercest competitor in mind allowing one's own performance to dictate complete control of the outcome. This was very appealing to a self-driven motivated competitor! I had been taught from a young age that the harder you work, the better you become. I liked the odds of my future and every outcome of every competition lying within my own personal pursuit. Team sports were fun and allowed a break in the intensity of the court, but my passion remained with the control of each outcome with the racquet in my hand. There was no teammate or partner to blame as I walked off the court following each match. And my destiny would be determined by my personal effort and the blame of each defeat would remain within the pages of my personal development. Tennis quickly progressed from an extra-curricular activity into a junior career. Traveling the country with my mother and coaches, this career would, in turn, pen the majority of the pages within my chapter of competition.

As this competition intensified, so did the lessons within my chapter. My dad, the protector, had also instilled more than the sense of security upon the pages of my life. He had taught me the importance of an incredible work ethic. He had introduced me to the secret to good luck. He always showed my siblings and myself that the harder you worked, the better luck you would achieve. He had provided security and love but set very high expectations for each of us. His expectation was simple. We give our very best and work our very hardest at everything we do. An expectation that was guided by His Word as stated in Colossians 3:23, "Whatever you do, work at it with all your heart, as working for the Lord, not for human masters."

That expectation molded me into the fiercest competitor that I could become and pushed me to test the limits of my ability. My mother would continue to whisper wisdom through my journey reminding me each step along the way that my ability was a true gift from God and that my effort and attitude would be my gift to Him. She is and continues to be, without question, an unstoppable driving force of strength, wisdom, comfort, and security.

"I don't know if I can do this" was a consistent phrase that swirled throughout my mind as my stomach would always turn.

Those personal thoughts of doubt and fear were consistently met with encouragement from two parents that believed I could do anything; or at least they made me think I could conquer the world. My mother was a powerful voice of strength, as she would always make me feel unstoppable with her impactful words of encouragement. Each word equipping me with the strength and courage needed to become my very best.

I would take a deep breath as I approached each and every competition with her words invading my mind. I learned to expect the harshest of constructive and lecturing debriefs following any exit off that court after a disappointing performance. A disappointing performance was never defined as a defeat but rather an embarrassing reflection of my effort, attitude, or approach. I learned quickly within my tour that my father was not the only one with expectations.

Following every match, a win was always celebrated; and a loss was debriefed yet comforted. But effort and ability were a non-negotiable expectation. As I grew in managing my fear, I began to focus on the performance and not the outcome. I began to enjoy the fight of the competition and not just the win. I was finding myself within the pages of my journey in competition and discovering to recognize the *joy* within the process. Early within the pages of my childhood, my desire to compete was accompanied by my fear of failure. Another aspect of my early childhood that was enslaved by the darkness of fear. There was an invaluable sense of comfort that enveloped my mother's every word. As we traveled the country together, she would fill the pages of my young athletic life with encouragement, confidence, and support pointing me to discover the blessing of *joy* found within the competition. And fueling much more than my athletic career, she was molding the very pages of my young life.

My tennis career and love of competition would propel me into a junior career that most would envy. A career that would claim numerous titles, rankings, and recruitment; but as I look back over the words scripted throughout this chapter, the blessing of *joy* was found in the many variables that propelled my success and failures through competition. From an early age, I was driven to succeed. But through this chapter of my life, I would learn about the requirements of finding true success. The discipline, the determination, the drive, the work ethic, the attitude, the commitment, the encouragement, and the sacrifice throughout this journey are where the true victory is found within the competition leading up to the win. The most impactful blessings of *joy* came through the tears of defeat as I realized early in my love for tennis—it was about personal development and betterment. It was about resisting the temptations of shortcuts or easy way outs. It was and continues to be about becoming the best version of myself. He calls us to more than we can imagine within each of our chapters, and my love for competition has propelled my quest of fulfilling His ultimate calling. A calling that appeals to the inner athlete in knowing that within this quest, we have already found victory within Him. I celebrate victoriously as a daughter of the one true King.

Upon this realization, this celebration just as I had learned from my own quest toward each individual win was not defined by just the end result of the outcome. It was defined by the journey upon the acceptance of our individual calling—one in which you would already claim victorious but one that would demand and require our recognition of the details of that requirement. Just as I had learned earlier within this chapter of competition, the true victory is found within the journey of competition leading to the ultimate win. George Bennard captured this recognition so beautifully within his popular hymn "The Old Rugged Cross" in 1912:

> So I'll cherish the old rugged cross
> 'Till my trophies at last I lay down
> I will cling to the old rugged cross
> And exchange it someday for a crown

As we sing this song over a century later, we celebrate in the victory won upon the cross but must recognize what this unimaginable sacrifice demands from our life. As discovered in my inner drive to win, this race with Christ requires the same discipline, determination, drive, work ethic, attitude, commitment, encouragement, and sacrifice throughout my journey; but at this finish line, my trophies are exchanged for my crown. Striving to finish a life with the ability to exclaim the words of 2 Timothy 4:7, "I have fought the good fight, I have finished the race, I have kept the faith."

*****

It was truly like looking in a mirror as her eight-year-old eyes differed only by the color. "Mom, I am playing!" she said as she fought back tears within the dugout.

"I know you are," I replied as she gathered up her glove and face mask and stormed the field to shortstop. I sat for a moment flooded by emotion from my childhood as I watched my youngest fight through the same emotions of competition that I had thirty years earlier. *I know exactly how you feel, baby girl,* I thought to myself as I watched her excel on the field. She was leading through her pain and giving everything she had as her team clenched the win advancing within the State

Tournament. Her chapter was just beginning as she turned this page within her own story, but I was filled with excitement at the recognition of the same blessing of *joy* that will be intertwined within her journey as she clings tight to the guidance of our Savior.

This journey within my chapter of competition has transformed my role in my children's quest to understand their own chapters of competition. All three of my children, differing in their approach, are all consumed with the drive of competition. My two sons are passionate about the future of their athletic careers and dream of where the success of each may take them. As I cheer them on in their incredible young efforts, I am conscious of the calling scripted throughout each of their pages as I recognize the joy of my new role. I pray that I may be a reflection of my own mother as I attempt to guide them in their own success of finding their joy in the midst of their individual competition, ultimately pointing all three to their most important victory in Him.

Chapter 5

SORROW

In the late pages of my personal journey of competition, I found myself battling a new pressure of decision-making. These decisions would shape my future and change the direction of my journey.

With an all-too-familiar persuasive smile, my friend and I would talk often about a possible visit to Ole Miss. It was what felt like, at the time, one of the most agonizing decisions my young brain could possibly interpret, but to him, it was clearly so simple! My very persuasive and quite stubborn friend had clearly made up his mind on the future of his collegiate golf career and was not so subtly trying to sway my decision on the future of my tennis career.

As a young athlete being actively recruited, the first of many decisions was the limitation of what school invitations to accept as an official visit. I was a competitive junior tennis player that had spent the majority of my teen years traveling this country and Europe playing tennis. As a top-ranked player, the recruitment process was intense. It was exciting but intense. I, at the time, had already made the decision that I was *not* going to attend a Mississippi university. The small-town girl trapped inside of my adventure-seeking body had bigger and better plans. Bigger and better simply meant "as far from small-town Mississippi as I could get!" So why in the world would I even entertain the thought of the offer on the table from Ole Miss?

Let me be clear. This incredibly profound decision of my seventeen-year-old brain to escape the great state of Mississippi was just the opposite of any well-thought-out decision. My entire story to this point had been so beautifully scripted within the corners of my small town, so I am unsure why my planned decision included something much different. My friend was a top-ranked junior golfer and had been experiencing the joy of recruitment due to the fact that he had already made his decision but sure was enjoying any trip north to Oxford. That being said, my friend was adamant about me taking this visit regardless of any decision that had or had not been made. He even organized for us to ride together on the planned weekend.

Needless to say, soon after, I was on the phone with the coaches confirming my official visit to the University of Mississippi. Not long after, we were headed north together for our weekend visit to Oxford, Mississippi. As we traveled north on I-55, he had big plans for the upcoming year. He talked of his well-thought-out plans involving golf, Greek life, football games, and fun while I talked of my other visits and experiences that had taken place and agonized over every detail of each. Decision-making had never been a strong point of mine. I would have much preferred God to simply mail me a letter with His choice, and I would have gladly followed that direction. This is a request that I had often hoped for but had never actually received that letter—I mean a physical letter with His penmanship offering guidance. I had frequently received His guidance through various channels but still so desperately sought that letter. I had so many thoughts swirling in my mind as we drove north, playing pros and cons on repeat through my very crowded-teenage mind. My friend had nothing but Hootie & the Blowfish, laughter, and carefree dreams on repeat. He always seemed to approach everything with that smile and ease, never taking anything too seriously. I, on the other hand, was tortured from the inside in my indecisive strive for perfection. Nevertheless, I was along for the ride and was looking forward to a weekend with friends. We both had several friends currently attending Ole Miss and several headed that direction the upcoming year. His girlfriend, also a close friend of mine, would be an upcoming freshman at Ole Miss in the fall; so this only fueled his desire to attend the University of Mississippi. So this weekend visit for him was purely going through the motion, but for me, it would quickly redirect my future.

Through the Ole Miss recruitment process, there were two appealing and consistently positive factors to the Lady Rebel Tennis Team—-Coach Montgomery and their record. Coach was, by first impression, the nicest, most friendly man that I had ever met. His approach to myself and my parents was off the chart and to be quite honest, a little too good to be true. I had mentioned to my friend that he was super interesting and seemed to be unrealistically kind! He seemed to approach every aspect of life through a similar lens of our shared Savior. Little did we know about the connection we would share with Coach and the impact he would have on our upcoming year of life!

The Lady Rebels were a fierce group of competitors, and although they happened to reside in the great state of Mississippi for the moment, they originated from all over the world. All but one were from outside the United States; and these girls were impressive, hard-working winners. I knew if I happened to end up among this group, I would be challenged and pushed to the limit. I knew and loved the overwhelming fact that these girls would make me better, and I also knew that with this combination of incredible players, we could become a dominant force at a high level. Winning was always an appealing quality, so with these two factors swirling in my mind, we pulled into beautiful Oxford, Mississippi.

Big-eyed and overwhelmed by emotion, we both went our separate ways to experience what would be an insanely exciting weekend. This place and these people were prepared to blow my mind with a magical glimpse of what the next years could entail. A standout Freshman Great was assigned the task of showing me a small glimpse into the reality of a Lady Rebel. I thought to myself, *oh, my word—these athletes are treated like royalty.* I would soon find out the reality of why each student athlete deserved every detailed advantage and red carpet rolled their way.

The weekend quickly came to an end, and the decisions quickly followed. I soon after signed with the University of Mississippi, and both of us jumped feet first into what would become an unimaginable freshman year.

As our freshman year flew by, we both were excited about heading back home for the summer. We settled back into small-town fun with our friends, enjoying summer classes at the local community college and late summer nights at the lake with our crew. We planned to meet at my house one afternoon. This was not any different than most summer nights as my house was one that our crew frequently gathered at on the lake. He had picked me up most days for class as we knocked out English Comp at the community college.

That night was different in one way—we had some friends in town from Ole Miss, and we were excited to all get together at a high school friend's house. So we met at my house, and out the door we flew for a fun summer night in small-town Mississippi. He and his girlfriend were trying to cheer me up as we headed to meet our friends! This summer had been one with several challenges. One of those challenges involved my high school sweetheart (and future husband, Jeff) and I back in the same small town together after a year of torturous *dating other people*. You see, my very persuasive and stubborn friend with his ever-annoying grin just happened to be my on-again/off-again boyfriend, Jeff's best bud! It was a complicated small-town lovers quarrel with my friend right in the middle, always directing us back together. Little did I know that this night, he had a plan of his own to redirect us back together once again. I secretly had a plan of my own, planning and hoping our entire crew would land at the same friend's house. The plan worked beautifully as the entire crew was back together with the addition of a few new friends from Ole Miss. The night was full of laughter, fun, and what seemed like endless smiles—everything a small-town summer night should encompass. As the night drew near to a close, I noticed that annoying-yet-ever-convincing grin as my friend talked with Jeff. He was clearly up to his redirection because as we begin to leave, I was now riding back to my house with Jeff. Before we left, we sang and danced to the great words of one last song by the Georgia Satellites.

With deep belly laughter and a swirl, we loaded up in separate cars. My friend flashed that winning, persuasive smile as we turned and loaded up to leave.

Windows down and music blaring, we rode the curvy roads of our small town as the warm summer air flowed through our hair. Incredibly happy because of my friend's redirection in carpool and to be reconnected with Jeff, we laughed and sang as we pulled into the entrance to my driveway. My friend, his girlfriend, and a couple of friends had left before us, and we were meeting back at my house. As I topped the hill leading down the entrance to my driveway, I heard something as we rode with our windows and sunroof open.

"Turn the music off," I said. Music continued to blare with everyone ignoring me. "Turn the music off!" I screamed.

As we turned the curve of my driveway, we were met with an unimaginable terror-stricken shrill. My friend's girlfriend was standing in the middle of my dark-wooded driveway. Slamming on brakes, the doors flew open. And we begin to race toward her in complete panic. As we ran to meet her, I can't help but frantically look around in what I think was indescribable shock.

She was injured but not making any sense! In an instant, a group of best friends were standing in the darkness of what seemed to be a nightmare amid screaming, confusion, and the realest form of fear I had ever imagined. The night air began to spin out of control as if everything around us was moving in fast-forward motion, but the six of us were stuck inside the moment with the inability to move. Jeff, myself, and one other friend began to run—faster than I knew my body was capable. We approached the small bridge connecting my long and curvy driveway and once again in slow motion. It was as if I was looking at reality through a slow motion camera, but my heart raced at a pace that was explosive! One side of the bridge had been demolished, and my friend's Explorer flipped upside down below the bridge with its headlight beam all that I can see. Standing in the middle of the darkness, I turned and looked back trying to understand the pieces of this slow-moving nightmare in the shadow of our abruptly stopped car's headlight. In that moment, I became sick—where was he? Turning back to the bridge, I saw Jeff and a friend had gone off the bridge in an attempt to rescue our friend. I began the sprint of a lifetime as I raced toward my house to call 911. Screaming as I ran approaching the house, my brother met me outside hearing the terror in my voice and stormed to the bridge to help in the rescue. As we waited for help, a small group of best friends frantically fought trying to save our friend. I returned to the bridge and climbed down to fight with Jeff and my brother who had both been tirelessly fighting in a desperate effort to save our friend. My brother pulled me out of the vehicle, throwing me to the bank. In utter shock, I sat shaking in terror as I watched the details unfold in front of me. In a matter of what seemed like years but was only minutes, our world had flipped into a living nightmare.

As emergency vehicles, ambulances, firefighters, and crew arrived at the scene, they forcefully removed me and my friends from the area. We were forced at that point to return to my house and wait. I stood in my kitchen wearing a muddy, wet red dress, peering into blank space in what I assume was pure shock. As I crumbled to a fetal position on the floor of my kitchen, I clenched both my legs and began to rock in utter fear followed by what felt like uncontrollable silent screams within my mind. I was trapped again—frozen in that moment with the inability to move. I was aware that there were people all around me. I could see and hear them as if they were a fast-moving whirlwind of water, but I was frozen within that movement. Help, please, someone, help—where was the *joy*? There was nothing but fear.

"It took Jaws of Life hours to get to him," a firefighter said. I was told it took hours for Jaws of Life to get to him as if that was supposed to make sense! The movement stopped, and I turned to the firefighter. "What did you say?"

He repeated himself, and then I asked, "Where is he?" In that moment, everything stopped. The firefighter grabbed my shoulders, looked me in the eyes, and said, "He didn't make it." Collapsing into his arms, I don't recall anything other than the tight embrace and my screaming into his wet T-shirt shoulder.

I don't remember much that was said beyond that moment, but I wish I could forget the sorrow and pain that invaded my being. I retreated to a corner in the dark space of my upstairs bedroom, desperately wanting to wake up from what seemed like a horror movie. My insides hurt like I did not know was possible, and every fiber of muscle within my heart was twisted in a gut-wrenching contortion. I did not know someone could experience such a depth of pain. I sat violently shaking in the corner of that room, a room that there was no possible joy. It did not exist in this horror.

As the sun began to rise the next morning, the light was not real. The horror had invaded and had a painful grip that cannot be articulated accurately. I was still trapped in a fast-moving nightmare yet frozen by unshakable fear. My friend's mother wanted to talk to me, so my parents and I headed toward their house. As my dad drove, I sat in the back seat still covered in mud but changed into a pair of shorts and T-shirt, staring blankly out the back windshield. I don't know if any words were spoken audibly on that long ride across town. If words were spoken, I do not remember audibly hearing the details of those words. I am still confused by the *reality* of these events. I don't want to go into the house. I don't remember anything other than tears. The tears that I saw in everyone's eyes, the tears that I could hear falling and being wiped away, and the tears that were streaming down my face in an uncontrollable flood. His mom sat in the back sunroom. With her own tears streaming, she grabbed me with a strong embrace. I felt numb and empty as I tried to answer all her questions as she desperately sought some form of answers to this unexplainable nightmare! After the questions concerning the accident, she wanted to discuss my friend's funeral arrangements. I, in this moment, still feel numb and trapped by fear as we discuss a list of guys that should be my friend's groomsmen one day, not his pallbearers.

Sorrow, deep pain, and confusion had quickly become the reality of my summer after freshman year. I did not know how to deal with it and could not wrestle away from the grip of its darkness. I was not sure I would ever be able to ride down my own driveway, much less return to Ole Miss or return to the normalcy of life. This sorrow would consume me and my thoughts—twisting and tormenting my mind with questions that had no answers or explanations. Where was the joy? There was none for me or anyone drowning with this level of sorrow. I could not see or feel any light resembling even the faintest flicker of hope, much less joy. I knew all the answers. I knew all the truth spoken from His word, and I knew that He had a specific plan.

> "'For I know the plans I have for you,' declares the Lord, 'Plans to prosper you and not to harm you, plans to give you hope and a future.'" (Jeremiah 29:11)

I was simply struggling with understanding that plan. And in the midst of my sorrow, I began searching for answers—answers that I never would receive. Why him? Why not me? As I returned to Ole Miss, I attempted to hold it all together. I would desperately cry out for help, and I would feel the Holy Spirit whisper within my soul; but I was drowning within my sorrow not able to even breathe. I was consumed. I knew from His Word that sorrow was part of reality, but *joy* should resound…

"A time to weep and a time to laugh, a time to mourn and a time to dance." (Ecclesiastes 3:4)

"Weeping may stay for the night, but rejoicing comes in the morning." (Psalm 30:5)

As the days turned into months, weeping continued; and sorrow grew thicker. There did not seem to be a time returning to laughter or dance, and I desperately sought the rejoicing that was to come in each morning. But each seemed to be vanquished by my questions and lack of understanding.

I was full of such unimaginable sorrow that was trapped inside a highly-functioning student athlete. I simply wanted to push rewind. Someone, help me start over. The guilt, the sadness, the anger, the what ifs, and the whys swirled rapidly within my mind. Jeff, my brother, and I had gone almost a complete year with no discussions of that night. It was too painful to talk about, but the pain and details of the night were drowning me from within at a rapid pace. I threw myself into an all-consuming quest for perfection through academics and athletics, but someone noticed my need for help. It turned out that my first impression of Coach a couple of years earlier on that official visit was absolutely true. His approach to myself and my parents was, in fact, off the chart and was not too good to be true. I remembered mentioning to my friend how he had seemed to be so unrealistically kind and how he seemed to approach every aspect of life through a similar lens of our shared Savior. It was through that lens of love that he guided me to seek help and begin the healing process through grief. My loving parents and my incredible coach constantly pointed me toward Him and guided me to seek the counsel I needed to begin healing. Through this counsel, I, for the first time, began to talk through the pain and confusion surrounding my sorrow. My pastor continued to encourage me to lay this burden at the cross, and He would take it from me—an action that I had convinced myself that I had already done repeatedly. The reality is that I had laid it down only to return each time to grab it back. Truth is that I did not really want to give it up. I was afraid that if I truly let it go, somehow I would lose all guilt, sorrow, and pain associated with the death of my friend as if that is what kept him close to me. The reality is that God was calling me to a higher form of sorrow—true Godly sorrow that provides real freedom and produces the *joy* that I was so desperately searching for amid my worldly sorrow.

"Godly sorrow brings repentance that leads to salvation and leaves no regret, but worldly sorrow brings death." (2 Corinthians 7:10)

As I laid my sorrow and confusion at the feet of my Savior, Jesus Christ, He truly took it from me and began a healing process in me that can only be described by His amazing love. When I truly let go, my joy was renewed through the Holy Spirit. I still hurt. I still had questions, and I still was confused; but the Holy Spirit within me battled daily on my behalf. My Savior took this all-consuming battle from within my soul, and He fought it and continues to fight it for me each day, month, and year providing light within my healing. That light focused on the joy that enveloped my friend's life and the incredible impact of his smile. A light shining a spotlight on the unforgettable joyful memories of my friend that will last a lifetime and drawing me away from the painful darkness of that night. I had allowed myself to get lost within my sorrow and allowed myself to be consumed by the confusion of unanswered questions rather than relying on the hope I have in Christ.

For those of us who know Christ as our personal Lord and Savior, there will be days of rejoicing again because the joy of the Lord is our strength. His strength is powerful enough to produce unexplainable joy amid even the darkest and most difficult pages of one's journey.

> "You turned my wailing into dancing; you removed my sackcloth and clothed me with joy, that my heart may sing your praises and not be silent. Lord my God, I will praise you forever." (Psalm 30:11–12)

I did not ever receive the answers to my questions, but I did receive my letter. Through my sorrow, I recognized *joy* in the life of my friend. My amazing friend lived a life cut short but a life lived full of abundance and carefree joy. A life that encompassed an infectious and impactful smile having incredible impact on all who knew him. A smile that would leave a lasting and unforgettable imprint upon the pages of my life and within my heart. I believe God used his life to pen the most beautiful letter of guidance to me, teaching me that though I may not always understand or agree with His plan—I will trust Him and the plan! I had gotten my letter! God continues to teach me that my hope and joy abide only in Him; and through each difficult or glorious step of this short journey called life, He is in control. The life of my friend reminded me to recognize the *joy* within each blessing of my life and encouraged me to approach each turn of a new page with an unforgettable and impactful smile. As I began to talk through the details of that horrific night, God began to also reveal two powerful examples of unrecognized *joy* within that very night of pain.

First I recognized the *joy* and blessing of my older brother's protection within that night of horror. Amid the chaos of his and Jeff's heroic effort to save our friend, my brother, without thought, protected me throughout the night. I was always bothered and even angered by the fact that he had physically and forcefully pulled me from the wrecked vehicle that night as I climbed in to try and help. Only later did I recognize the *joy* within that moment of protection. My brother was protecting me from the painful details within that vehicle. My brother would continue to provide an umbrella of protection that would shade every page of my journey. As God revealed this truth to me within the healing process, I was overwhelmed by the recognition of the *joy* within the blessing of a brother that would arguably be one of the most incredible humble heroes within my world.

Second was the insanely intense love that was exuded from my then on-again/off-again boyfriend in his selfless attempt to save our friend. Jeff was always one who loved bigger than life, investing and genuinely caring on a personal level with each acquaintance. But Jeff's love for his friends was unmatched. People have always been drawn to him, and the secret of that attraction was beginning to be revealed to me. It was the size of his heart—undoubtedly and arguably the largest of his time. Through this sorrow, God revealed yet another incredible *joy* in the blessing of Jeff. As my friend had so eagerly directed us back together, I ultimately found another immeasurable source of *joy* in Jeff— as he would choose to love me and my future family for the rest of our life. He loves us with the same reckless abandonment that I had witnessed that night as he fought for our friend, and I witness it daily as he strives to love as we are called to love—as our Savior loves. I am reminded frequently through the lyrics of "Live Like That" by Sidewalk Prophets of the important calling on our life to simply love. Jeff encompasses this level of love, and I cling tight to the recognition of the blessing from this *joy* as I navigate through the journey of any sorrow this short life may throw our way. And as this song plays frequently, tears always stream as I am overwhelmed with the many blessings of my Savior's love.

Another recognition of *joy* written in my letter of life; penned so beautifully using the life of our great friend. I will always stand with my hands stretched high praising my Savior forever for the *joy* I have in Him and for the penmanship of my letter. A letter pointing to the truth exclaimed in this verse of Psalm 16, "You make known to me the path of life; in your presence there is fullness of joy; at your right hand are pleasures forevermore."

Chapter 6

MARRIAGE

"It starts with an 'M'," he says as we talk on the phone.

It was a game we had begun to play each night as we talked for hours. The game consists of simply telling each other the letter of our secret crush. Living next door, Jeff and I had become inseparable. We had built our house on the lake my tenth-grade year, placing Jeff and me right next door to each other. We were each other's person, telling each other the secrets of our teenage heart. For years, I had dated Jeff's best friend, and I had orchestrated his various dates. During the weekend, roaming the roads together on double dates, only to return home to the lake with laughter and stories of each encounter.

Lately, something had begun to change, and something was different. I noticed with each discussion of who his next date should be, a strange sense of emotion would overcome me. I quickly was noticing him differently, and I was starting to think he may feel the same way too. We were beginning to tread into uncharted waters, and our friendship seemed to be changing.

"His name starts with a 'J'," I replied with a sense of nervousness.

It was quite silly the way we proceeded, but it was a safe way to test the waters. I had currently been dating a boy that just happened to have a name that started with J, and he had been dating a girl whose name started with an M, so the responses would safely lend to each of our imagination. This silly and ridiculous game of crush spelling lasted for several weeks, discussing it at detail each night over the phone, but at school each day, we would return to our best friend status as if nothing had been discussed.

One night after studying together for an upcoming test, things changed rapidly. Jeff likes to tell the story that I laid one on him, but the truth was slightly different than he explains. While leaving that night from my house, I simply stood in front of his car door, forcing him to make a decision…that decision would change the course of our future with one kiss.

Scared of losing our best friend, Jeff and I tormented ourselves with the decision to date or remain best friends. While at school we distanced ourselves with the awkwardness that followed our first kiss. We quickly moved past the uncertainty and started an adventure that seven years later would end in marriage. Those seven years would be a complicated and challenging several years within our journey.

Two years full of proms, homecomings, ball games, and more flew by as we approached graduation and goodbyes. I had signed with Ole Miss to play tennis, and he had signed with SMCC to play basketball. Due to these decisions placing four hours in between us, we came to a conclusion that we would remain close friends and step into collegiate life with the ability to date other people. It would, in turn, become the most torturous few years that one young heart could imagine. As he and I both would date other people on occasion, we would continue to talk every day, and the agony that each of us was ensuing on another was terrible. After a tough freshman year, our sophomore year brought upon more change. We decided not to talk because the heartache that it was causing between the two of us was not fair or healthy for anyone involved.

For the first time in years, my best friend was absent, and there was an extreme void within my being. Amid a difficult year of healing from the tragedy of losing our friend, looking back, it was horrible timing to distance ourselves. The pain of the event was too great to discuss, so possibly another reason we decided to quit communicating.

Jeff and I quickly discovered that the distance and silence were too much to handle, and began to resume our daily talks and would see each other with every return home. We were both still too stubborn to admit our desire to solely see each other, so we continued this torturous relationship/friendship for the next couple of years. Soon after, finding ourselves at another crossroads facing the same decision. We once again decide poorly, cutting communications the summer prior to our senior year. Another summer that would quickly redirect our lives. Living in Oxford that summer, studying hard to prepare for the upcoming reattempt at improving my MCAT score, I kept myself quite busy.

Jeff was enjoying his summer as a lifeguard living in Hattiesburg attending Southern MS. Once again, we had made the decision not to speak the remainder of the summer, so my stubborn prideful self was determined to honor that agreement no matter the circumstance. One Sunday, a friend and I were sitting in church when I was overcome with sickness, and as my stomach turned, I looked at my friend to state that I thought something was wrong. Leaving church, I told my friend maybe I just needed to rest, so I decided to take an afternoon nap before heading to the library. As I lay down in my room, the phone rang, and it was my mother.

"Missy, we are headed to Hattiesburg. Jeff has been in an accident and is being taken into surgery now."

Confused, I began to ask many questions that she could not answer. I jumped into my SUV and began my emotional journey south. The specific details of terror and confusion that swirled through my mind as I drove south that day are unclear and crowded within my memory, but the intensity of the emotion is quite vivid. Upon arrival, an all too familiar whirlwind of slow-motion chaos began to invade the circumstances of uncertainty. The waiting room and hallways of that hospital were crowded, and Jeff was concluding the first of many surgeries.

Although I don't remember my exact thoughts, with so much emotion flowing through my mind, I must have been thinking about the stupid decision for us not to talk and frustrated over our selfish pride. I can only imagine the sense of hope within my flooded heart for another chance. As the doctor walked out, he stated many details of Jeff's condition that I don't recall. The memory of that discussion is crowded within the emotion of the moment. It appeared that Jeff was stable but would have a long road ahead of him. He had been hit head on in the car accident, and his legs endured extensive damage. The specific details of what followed that moment are unclear within my memory, but the redirection of our relationship had a lasting impact.

Leaving summer school, I returned home to help with Jeff's care as Jeff would have multiple surgeries over the next year in his process of healing, and we would each regain our best friend. The pain and suffering that Jeff endured are indescribable, but the joy hidden within the pages of this difficult year is immeasurable. Another traumatic event within our lives had been used by God to rewrite the direction within our relationship. A chapter within each of our personal journeys that God would use to reveal such beautiful joy within our friendship. An event, upon looking back, that scripted an incredible recognition of the powerful danger associated with any stubborn pride or ambition. As scripture challenges us in chapter two of Philippians, we are to do nothing out of selfish ambition or vain conceit but rather in humility, valuing others above ourselves.

Often, our human sin-filled nature deceives us into believing our own value is more important than others. This deceit causing us to approach each and every relationship with a false sense of entitlement. That selfish approach produces an unhealthy barricade to what God has so beautifully called us to within any relationship. This barricade limiting the very blessing of joy God so graciously wants to produce within every honoring relationship of love. Pride ultimately not only barricading the potential of a beautiful relationship but ending many tragically for those who do not recognize the danger. God leading and teaching us to put others needs above our own, allowing a relationship to prosper into something that can only be scripted by our Creator. I would not have chosen the sequence of events within this painful chapter, but am grateful for the lesson in pride and the recognition of joy within their very pages.

Two years later, a proposal would follow, and Jeff and I would begin a new adventure as I married my best friend. As a child, I was never into the fairy tales or prince charming. I was blessed with a real-life example of what marriage was designed to look like on a daily basis through the loving example of my parents. I had never dreamed of prince charming or never desired to become a princess. I simply had prayed for a real-life love resembling my incredible father. Little did I know that God's plan would include the boy next door, and little did I know, the dream of which life with him would provide.

I have recognized and continue to recognize the daily blessing of JOY within Jeff. He loves with no comparison, and he chooses to love me. For seventeen years, Jeff and I have and continue to have the ride of a lifetime. Experiencing the hurdles of life together, attempting to embrace each encounter through the lens of His guidance. Marriage is indeed an obstacle course requiring a committed team, not the fairy tale with the effortless happy ever after. God revealed early within our marriage the necessity of selfless teamwork. A secret to our awesome but not perfect marriage lies within a daily choice to put each other's need before our own. A constant quest to make the other happy, recognizing their source of utmost joy varies differently than our own. It was an early revelation as we continued to grow together and seek to understand each other's greatest needs. Each of these needs important to the success of finding our joy.

Also, recognizing that it is not easy and requires a constant commitment to hard work is one of the most important requirements to finding real joy. Communicating through the happy moments, but more importantly, talking together through the difficult ones. As life progresses, kids are welcomed, and careers progress these simple tasks of finding marital bliss become more complicated, and time together more crowded—but as God has revealed through us, it is not impossible. His desire is greater than any struggle we may face, and our ability to recognize His desire produces the lasting JOY of our successful marriage. My amazing grandmother penned it so beautifully in a poem she had written in 1937, titled, "Happiness for Two." She exclaimed the necessity to fight for the happiness found in love.

Happiness for Two

Life to me is something great
Not of fame and sorrows few
But of dearer joys and hearts content
Is life to me with you.

I weave a pattern of life with you
Evenings precious with perfect bliss
Pleasant rooms where laughter rings
And the warm devoted kiss

Homeward at the close of day
You will find me at one door
With outstretched arms and smiling face
For you to caress and kiss and adore

Worries you have put aside

For there's supper just for two

We pray to God that this will last

And that there are always sorrows few

I'll do the dishes in a hurry

For us to be together again

We'll count stars one by one

Maybe there won't be but ten

Life can always be this way

Happiness will forever be

As long as we fight for it

And will have won the victory

—Toodles Dickerson

My grandmother recognized early within her marriage the necessity of fighting for love orchestrated by Him. Our society would like for you to believe that when it gets dark, you leave;

when you're not happy, you leave. There is nothing further from His truth, and His desire is for each of us to find extreme JOY within our marriage and allow Him to guide us through each page of our chapter.

In Ephesians 4:2, God calls us to "Be completely humble and gentle; be patient, bearing with one another in love." God does not promise each relationship is a fairy tale with endless days of perfection, but He calls us through humility and patience to allow His love to conquer each challenge upon our page. Our marriage has not been one of complete perfection; it has been one of complete commitment. A commitment allowing our love of Christ to guide and direct our fight for each other and our love through our marriage. As my grandmother penned, the fight leads to the victory in love. There have been difficult moments within our wonderful seventeen years of adventurous marriage. One moment, in particular, where time would stand still, and reality would choke us to our being. A moment where three audibly spoken words rocked us to our core, but a moment that God used to help us recognize the great need of each other to achieve real joy.

As we celebrated the marriage of a niece amid the happiness that occurs within a family wedding, we experienced one of those moments. That weekend was composed of such happiness defined by the outside eye looking in, but exploited by the mistakes within our personal choices. As we checked into the hotel with our three kids after traveling several hours, one can only imagine we were already flustered by the banter that occurs on such family road trips.

"He's looking at me. She's touching me. He took my iPad," whined from the mouth of each of my three for what seemed like an eternity.

Not many words were spoken between Jeff and I on that drive except the usual details of "Did we have all the kids' clothes?" "Had we packed all the needed equipment for the upcoming ball tournament?" And the "Are you going to handle this?" on repeat. Dragging our stuff into the hotel room, we both sat and looked at each other in exhaustion. With a deep breath, I began to instruct everyone within that room to get it together. We were needed dressed and looking our best for the rehearsal dinner in a short time.

As we arrived at the church for the rehearsal, we were greeted by family and friends both exclaiming what a beautiful family and children we had. And for a brief passing moment, I reveled in the fact that I had done a pretty good job in putting my good-looking family together! Distracted by all the hustle and bustle that goes along with the rehearsal and by chasing our flower girl around as we ensured she was in the correct spot, I was quickly brought back to our overwhelming sense of family chaos.

We successfully made it through the rehearsal and rehearsal dinner and appeared to have it all together—quite closely to perfection according to all the praises that we heard throughout the night. Patting myself on the back once again, we load back up, and we head back to what would become a difficult night within that hotel room. Surrounded by what appeared to be such happiness and joy as my oldest slept clenching his new way-too-expensive bat, my middle asleep close by with his cowlick in rare form, and my youngest out with a head full of curls in preparation for her big day, I smile with contentment at my little crew in all their glory.

Jeff turns to me in that very crowded hotel room and utters three words that would rock me to my core. He simply states, "I'm not happy." Not in an I am not happy and want to leave or want out of this, but a cry of desperation from the neglect that our chaotically busy life had ensued. I was utterly speechless, as within an unexpected moment, my heart filled with quicksand, and I began to sink within myself. Lying in bed for what felt like an eternity, thoughts raced through my head, and heartbreaking reality crept in quickly. How could we have gotten to this point within a marriage that outwardly would appear near perfection? How could I have put what innocently had seemed like my responsibility in front of the needs of the most important relationship, outside of my relationship with Christ, and calling upon my life?

The weekend continued, and we, as usual, looked like what most would describe as picture perfect, but inside, the reality was heart wrenching. We both wanted more, and my husband was man enough to speak truth into our relationship. We had allowed our kids, their schedule, and our careers to infiltrate the very space designed for our marriage. Each of these things being good at their core, and blessings within themself, but destructive when placed in front of the need of each other. God calls us to love each other as He loves the church. Wow, He sent His one and only Son to die for the church and loves us with an unconditional and undeserving love.

In the English Standard Version of Ephesians 4:2–3, the verses instruct us to, "With all humility and gentleness, with patience bearing with one another in love, EAGER to maintain the unity of the Spirit in the bond of peace." In that heart-pounding moment of truth while lying in the quiet dark hotel room, I recognized that I had been EAGER to perfect all things within my life excluding the most important need that I am called upon—my beautiful, kind, God-loving husband! Consciously and consistently placing Jeff's needs in front of my kids, myself, and our schedules would need to immediately repair itself to rectify the distance within our marriage. Jeff and I both needed to quickly return to the calling God had placed within our marriage, learning to enjoy the chaos of our kids and career, only to take a backseat to our marriage and each other. The joy recognized in the boldness of my husband's love is unmatched, and we quickly returned to the bliss of each other and the whirlwind of what life with three young kids entailed.

The truth found within this reality is important. This truth revealing the endless, and at times tested need to keep this a priority, is a continuous challenge. As life continues to crowd the sacred space intended for our marriage, one must actively choose to barricade this space for only each other. This is an ongoing battle and war as Jeff and I attempt to defend the space intended for only each other. Our children, careers, and our selfish desires often try to creep within this protected space— requiring a constant choice to battle through these obstacles to find a successful defense strategy leading to the victory found in love. The truth within a real marriage is that this commitment takes work and constant effort. As my grandmother penned, the victory of love is found within the fight. If a verbal agreement was stone proof, our nation would be experiencing a much different marriage survival rate. The initial verbal commitment of "for better or for worse" is simply an acknowledgment that your spouse is worth this fight! The commitment takes daily effort in an ongoing and increasingly difficult battle—a battle that is worth it! It is never a "one-and-done" acknowledgement or conversation in this commitment—it is a lifetime approach, leading to the genuine joy found within a "fought-for" marriage.

As time passed, schedules intensified, and years of pages would turn, we would often find ourselves in a similar whirlwind of life and expectations. Our oldest had traded his baseball bat in for basketball shoes and football cleats. My middle had begun dreaming of his future as the next Larry Bird, and our daughter had picked up a bat of her own. Needless to say, we were back to moving in fast motion, and quickly had become consumed by color-coded practice and game schedules, softball tournaments, football workouts, basketball practices, Sunday school teaching schedules, youth trips, summer reading, and much more.

Throughout our fast-moving journey, I would often find myself back in that same moment within the hotel room, reminded of the paralyzing fear of what felt like quicksand settling within my chest. Now adding a swirl of color-coded schedules swimming in my mind similar to the Willy Wonka boat ride, I would struggle often to balance my priorities.

Quiet within our room one night, we discussed the continuous struggles within our whirlwind, remembering those same three words that had transformed our effort and acknowledging the reality of the continuous struggle. Discussing the bravery it takes to communicate a heart of hurt, but the disaster that follows a hurting heart of silence. Discussing the joy we find in our relationship through the ability we had to courageously and honestly call each other out if our priorities ever began to slip. Coming a long way from the hours of playing a silly, ridiculous game of crush spelling, we now had the trusting relationship of open communication. We had learned and continue to learn that silence drives distance between our relationship.

Remembering that moment back in that hotel room, I had often thought to myself, *I wonder if my father had ever uttered those words to my mother and had my mom ever struggled with balancing her whirlwind.* Instantly, I recognized it really didn't matter because even if they had, as we had, they obviously had discovered the way to work through all challenges recognizing the secret to finding real JOY within a marriage as they exuded its beauty daily within their example. Jeff consistently reminds me through his unconditional love, the importance of keeping all our swirling pieces of our whirlwind behind each other—not allowing ourselves to get back to that spot.

One night as we had discussed our never-ending whirlwind and the power of those three words, Jeff looked at me with his beautiful blue eyes and said, "If we both put the amount of time and effort into our marriage that we put into coaching our kids sports teams, could you imagine the marriage we could have daily?"

I had no words as I peered through his clear blue eyes as the reality of that truth was resounding. We both too often allow time to pass and activities to invade the space between both of us! We both actively chose at times to exhaust all our effort toward everything within our whirlwind, forgetting that with each effort we pushed more things in front of each other. These, once again, things that are far from harmless and within themselves great important parts of our life, but these things were crowding the very space designed for our relationship.

Silence invaded but was followed by love and eagerness. A sense of peace that can only come from our heavenly Father, one that cannot be explained. As we lay in our bed discussing our failures and neglect, we realized within that moment that we had talked for hours about only us…we were overcome with a JOY that is indescribable. A JOY that came from our Savior's desire. We both often strive so hard to perfect everything within our world that we allow this strive for perfection to drive a wedge between our relationship. A relationship that takes work and effort, a relationship that is challenging, and at times exhausting, but a relationship when approached through our Saviors eyes and lived out according to His desire, is the most earthly rewarding relationship within any chapter upon this journey. We are committed to keeping each other's needs in front of any other priority in our life. Our kids are the most important three human beings in my world, but they each come after their amazing father. I have learned and continue to learn that real authentic JOY is found in our relationship when and only when it is guided by both of our daily efforts to ultimately grow in our relationship with Christ.

In doing this correctly and consciously, each day I fall more in love with Jeff. God uses each moment to reveal to me how incredibly blessed I am through Jeff. As a child, I had never dreamed of prince charming but had longed for someone to love me and my future children as I had experienced my father love my mom and myself. God placed him right next door, and he would become more than I could ever have imagined, dreamed, or hoped for in a husband. God knew how stubborn I was in my need for clarity within decision making, so he literally placed Jeff next door. A childhood best friend that would grow into an incredible man of God, husband, and father. I am loved like I do not deserve, I am cared for like no other, and I am truly experiencing the genuine JOY that God desires within a marriage. Jeff Carruth's worth is immeasurable, and I, through the guidance of my Savior, will live each day rejoicing in that JOY with him. Together we face each day with a choice to put each other first, and together we make that commitment finding our JOY.

Chapter 7

MOTHERHOOD

My pages seem to turn at the most rapid pace within the crazy adventure of motherhood, an adventure that continues to provide intense learning with every flip. I am actively pursuing an attempt to find the pause button within this chapter of my journey. One in which I have not quite figured out nor do I claim to have found all the answers. These pages providing not only the most rapid pace of turns but some of the most joy-filled moments within the journey.

We were crowded within our small upstairs bathroom as we waited patiently for the blue-and-white stick to digitally provide one of the most exciting yet terrifying words that would be scripted across the pages of the day. The day that changed the course of direction more than either one of us could ever imagine. "Pregnant!" I screamed and jumped for what must have been minutes stretched into an eternity of bliss! Jeff and I both ecstatic and in shock!! Oh my goodness. Is this right? We laughed, cried, and jumped only to continue asking that same question to ourselves repeatedly. Could this be right? Do you think this is really right? So unsure of the clarity, we choose to jump in the car and drive to the nearest drug store. We raced up and down the aisle within the drug store examining each brand and type of pregnancy test and loaded a basket full and raced giddily to the check out. Dumping several boxes of pregnancy test across the counter, we, excited in our young quest for pregnancy, would proceed to spend a ridiculous amount of money on additional pregnancy tests to really confirm the news. We had to purchase the more expensive digital brand to ensure the accuracy because in our mind, we were convinced the stripes may be inaccurate! So minutes later, we found ourselves sitting in a bathroom covered in small blue-and-white sticks all reading *pregnant*!

A couple of weeks later, the question of the reality of pregnancy would need no confirmation! The small bathroom upstairs had been ridded of all the blue-and-white test sticks and replaced by the constant sounds of distress. The bliss was gone, and the vomiting would not stop. *Is this normal?* I thought on multiple occasions as I found myself next to the toilet.

"This will end soon," so many would say but soon was nowhere in sight. I had heard so many people talk of the incredible joy they had found within their pregnancy. Those people were all clearly lying. I could find no joy amid the vomit and constant turning of my stomach. This was insane, but everyone assured me this sickness would pass. Actually, most would share that it was just *morning sickness.* I soon realized that these people had also lied! It was in no way shape or form a morning sickness. This was an all-out never-ending sickness! Books and others would attest to the majority of all sickness ending after the first trimester. This too was developing into another lie!

"Would anyone around me speak any truth into me about the invasion occurring within my body?" I asked myself on several occasions while hugging whatever toilet I happened to be able to get to at the moment. Jeff was absolutely frightened of me, my mood, and the never-ending dry heaving. I am telling you the words that were covering the beginning pages of this chapter were anything but joy-filled. I was filled with nothing but nausea and exhaustion!

"I am going to have you walk the halls for a bit, and let's see if your labor progresses. We may be having a baby today!" my doctor said as she smiled with relief. Relief due to the fact that she knew the wrath that may have exploded from within my two hundred pounds had she not uttered those words. *Oh, I am going to walk these halls all right,* I thought to myself as Jeff and I headed up and down the halls of the hospital. Still feeling anything but joy, pain was shooting down my right leg as I would clench Jeff's hand and squeeze as hard as I possibly could. For some sick reason, I had convinced myself if I caused Jeff a small level of pain within that moment, it would somehow make me feel better. I had officially turned into someone crazy, but I was determined I was not leaving until someone at that hospital got this baby out of me that day. Hours later, I had received my epidural; and for the first time in nine months, I actually felt all right! I could see light at the end of the tunnel, and our excitement grew as we waited patiently for our baby boy to make his arrival. Our families had flooded the hospital, filling the waiting room and halls with more people than allowed. We were all ecstatic about the arrival of our new addition.

We had made an early decision that my mom would be with us in the delivery room. Jeff was and is not the best at dealing with blood or even the slightest sight or sound of medical procedures. Previously passing out while I received an IV was just a confirmation that I may need an additional support system. Not to mention, my mom (the comforter) was needed within the room to greet her first grand baby! Almost thirteen hours after arriving at the hospital, it was time to push. Overcome with a combination of fear and excitement, the events began to unfold. With Jeff facing the wall (completely facing the wall), my mom at my side, and my doctor and my sister in between the stirrups, I begin to push on command. Oh yes—within the excitement of the moment, my fearless younger sister had managed her way not only into the delivery suite but in between the stirrups right over the shoulder of my physician. As my physician would say push, Kristen proceeded to echo her command! "Push," my doctor would command followed by "Push," my sister would chime in.

"You are doing great, Missy!" my doctor would explain. Easy for her to say, I did not feel like I was doing great. Once again, there was a chime in from my sister, "Great one, Missy. I can see his head." First of all, how does she know that was a *great one?* And secondly, who let her in here! Nurses had placed an oxygen mask on my face to assist with breathing, so I was having trouble communicating; but my sister was not! I can remember thinking, *If I could get this foot out of my stirrup, I would smoke her right in the face!* With Jeff still looking at the wall, my mom at my side, and my sister appearing to assist my physician, I had been pushing for a couple of hours. Exhausted, I started to notice concern within the nurses' faces.

"One more push, Missy! You can do this!" my doctor said. And with that, I gave it all I had left. In that instant, things changed. I heard my doctor state the time and call for help. Jeff looked concerned. My sister had removed herself, and I could see my mother had retreated to the couch to pray. Confused with the fast-moving pieces within the moment, I was unaware of the danger that was occurring. Apparently, my baby boy had turned as his head was being born causing his shoulders to lodge him within the exit. It is called shoulder dystocia and only allowed minutes to deliver with safety. Within seconds, the incredible medical team had acted quickly and efficiently, saving my beautiful firstborn and providing me with the first real moment of God's blessing of *joy* through parenthood. As I held my beautiful baby boy, in that instant, I understood the brevity of the prayer my mother lavished upon me from the time of my conception as I would continue to pour that same prayer of hope over my precious son.

Seventeen months later, we would find ourselves back in that small bathroom staring at that same digital reading—pregnant! Ecstatic about the reading of that blue-and-white stick, Jeff and I could not believe it. We were going to have another baby as we were still operating on the pure adrenaline of raising a one-and-a-half year old! The anticipation, excitement, and joy were met quickly with the all too familiar return of agonizing sickness. But this time, no lying mothers or books would deceive me in what the reality of these next several months would entail!

Being much more prepared and with the history of my previous birth, we were super excited about the plan of a scheduled C-section! Leaving the office that day, we had our plan in place; and I liked it. In one week, we would welcome our second baby boy into our family. Room was ready, bags packed, and name picked for our new addition as we eagerly got ready for the day. Even the grandparents had come over the day before due to fact of the early scheduled procedure and an incoming storm in the gulf. Hurricane Katrina was approaching landfall on the coast that morning, but we knew we should be fine seeing that we lived about 70 miles north of the coast.

Within hours, our small fear of possibly losing power had escalated to fear of losing lives. As I sat under the stairs holding my two-year-old son and feeling the pounding kicks of my unborn, losing power was the least of our worries. Terrified of the noises and chaos that quickly ensued, I could hear trees snapping and crashing against our home. In those intense moments, I was overcome with the reality of what was taking place. We were experiencing what would quickly be known as one of the most damaging storms that this area would ever endure. When hours of intensity had begun to pass, the reality of a bigger storm quickly set in within the walls of our home. It was time for this baby, and we were not sure that we could get out of this neighborhood.

Neighborhood heroes would emerge within the streets of our south Mississippi community working together to ensure everyone's safety and in an effort to get me to the hospital. Men with chainsaws and trucks would cut an escape from our neighborhood leading to an already crowded road of utility trucks. Emergency personnel were out in forces, and as we slowly proceeded through an obstacle of trees and debris, we could not believe what our eyes would see—devastation throughout our town. Distracted by the damage momentarily, we managed to make it to the hospital. It was a war zone of its own. No power and no water led to an immediate evacuation of any and all emergencies including upcoming surgeries or planned deliveries. It was not possible for me to have a natural delivery due to the complications of my previous birth, and there was no water or power, meaning that there was no sterile equipment to provide any safe procedure. I was faced with a dilemma as I had an unborn baby ready to make his entrance. Looking back upon the words scripted throughout these pages, my mighty God was creating an unexplainable masterpiece on our behalf. By the time we had returned to our house, I would be on a cell phone with an *ob-gyn* from a couple hours away in a small town just north of our parents' home. And soon after obtaining much sought-after gas, we were on our way to a small town hospital two hours away as this doctor awaited our arrival. He was an incredible doctor who prepared to deliver our new baby in a place that we had not planned but one that would become an incredible blessing of *joy* within our pages of this unimaginable journey. A journey that would end with the most beautiful 10-pound baby boy that you had ever seen. Perfectly healthy and full of bright red hair, he exuded the reminder of how amazing our heavenly Father was in orchestrating his incredible arrival. Looking within my newborn son's eyes, His love for us was so evident within this beautiful baby boy. And just as with my firstborn, I continued to lavish the same prayer of hope over his life.

It would be almost four years later that we would repeat our excitement within this chapter as we prepared to welcome, this time, a beautiful baby girl. I felt as if our world was complete hearing the news of the addition of a girl. Always praying for each unborn child to be blessed with good health and development, we would be elated with the news of adding some pink to our home. I had always expected a house full of boys with our sports-loving household—but secretly could not contain my excitement to welcome our little girl. As her birth would not involve the intense circumstances or obstacles that her brothers' arrivals ensued, her entrance into this world would introduce a new depth of motherhood. I would begin to pour out the same prayer upon her life as her brothers, praying for her to come to the saving knowledge of our Lord and Savior recognizing her true *joy* in Him. While admiring the beauty and pink bow of my one-day-old newborn, a knock would rattle the door.

"Come in," I said as I continued the admiration. "I am a pediatric cardiologist, and I am here to walk through the details of your daughter's heart," he said without hesitation. I remember him talking but could not process the words that were coming out of his mouth. He began to describe the multiple defects that had been found within her heart. He talked so calmly as if he was discussing the color of her hair. Her hair, by the way, was a deep dark brown; but her heart, apparently, had several issues. I shook my head as if I understood the terms he was describing. And before I knew, he had turned to walk out the door. I turned to look at my visitors within the room, and with tears strolling down my face, I attempted to ask for some explanation of the event. It would be one of many moments within this chapter that I felt completely overwhelmed. The hormones, I am sure, compounded my inability to process the news and my inability to stop the tears. I was trapped within the moment lacking full understanding. Fear would attempt to rear its ugly head and invade with darkness, but our God shielded me and my beautiful daughter from its aggressive lies. Philippians 4:6–7 reminding me:

"Do not be anxious about anything, but in
every situation, by prayer and petition, with
thanksgiving, present your requests to God.

And the peace of God, which transcends all understanding, will guard your hearts and your minds in Christ Jesus."

I knew that I had no need for fear as my God was bigger than any issue we may face and that He would battle and protect on her behalf. As time would pass, I would come to the understanding of her condition. She, in fact, was born with multiple defects and holes within her heart each with the possibility of closing within time and repairing themselves. This is another example found within these pages of how God's hand is upon every minute detail of our being, as our beautiful daughter would be completely dismissed from her pediatric cardiologist by the time she was five. Her life was blessed with perfect health and no limitations. Our God continued to amaze with His abundant blessings poured throughout this chapter of our journey.

The simple joys found within the moments of motherhood could fill unlimited lines with beautifully scripted words of joy. The pages would be endless as I described every moment of joy that I recognize upon each face of my children. There seems to be a common thread scripted throughout each chapter of my journey—that thread weaving moments of joy found within the simplicity of life. Every recognized moment creating electric explosions within my heart. Explosions that feel like a private Fourth of July inside my soul, producing ripples of electric joy. These fireworks serving as a defibrillator shock within my heart regenerating me to be more consistent in my recognition of the amazing beauty found within these simple moments. Let's be honest, sometimes we can miss these moments as we are blinded by the routine; or possibly just exhausted by our efforts. These moments are what fuel my focus and redirect my efforts. The joyful blessings produced through the simplicity of life are the moments I am determined not to miss. I am committed to avoid the distraction of the grandiose that this world defines as parenting success, and rather determined to focus on the beauty within the simple moments of motherhood. A journey that is filled with so many exciting pages filling multiple chapters that are being flipped at such a rapid pace. As I strive to notice every simple but important moment within my children's life, I am reminded that each is a blessing from Him. I need no bumper sticker or social media post to describe their greatness, I see it daily within the individual moments of their life. I can see it within the confidence of my oldest as he leads with admirable courage. I discover and hear it through a cell phone check embedded in the words of encouragement in a text to his friend. I can feel it when he smiles the same crooked smile as his dad, loving his family and friends as impactful as his father. I see it in the authenticity of my middles bright blue eyes, as he listens and cares with genuine, authentic interest to all who know him. I can hear it in the never ending movement of his feet, as he shuffles with an endless effort giving over a hundred percent in everything he does. I can feel it when he turns around each day as he walks out the door to ensure I heard him as he says he loves me too. I hear it within my daughter's laughter, a deep belly laughter that causes the room to move. I can see it within the movement of her eyes as she expressively discusses the excitement found within her day. I can feel it as she grabs my hand at night to ensure I don't leave her too soon, just as I would grab the hand of my own mother.

These three are not perfect, but God is creating beautifully perfect moments of joy through their amazing lives, and I am determined not to miss even one of them! Within each chapter of life, we have a choice to realize and recognize the joy scripted throughout the moving pages within ones journey. These pages are too important to be missed or skimmed through, they hold an incredible calling of responsibility. This responsibility producing the most unimaginable joy found within the words of the pages scripted and guided by Him.

I am reminded through the realization and recognition of such simple but powerful moments of joy found within motherhood, that we so often spend our misguided time as parents striving to perfect so many other things within our children's life. These things filled with a success defined by the outside world, serving as temporary and tempting distractions in our overall calling as a parent. Things that fill both their world and ours with moments of self-worth and admiration—but moments that all fade within time. I sometimes find myself consumed and trapped within the demands of their athletic, academic, and personal success, and I am often guilty of becoming blinded within the misleading demands of this time-consuming focus. I am consistently redirected to the reminder recognized within my own life—one's genuine joy is found only within Him. The joy that is intertwined within the personal, earthly success of each of my children is found within the blessings of His plan for them. Genuine joy is only produced from within a spiritual journey in Him. Each of the earthly successes found within this chapter provide fun but fleeting moments of happiness within this life, so we must be reminded and challenged to focus our effort on improving our reflection of Him through each and every successful chapter. This reflection and guidance pointing our children toward Him, as we strive to live out our calling found in Proverbs 22:6.

The significance of this calling defines a chapter of incredible responsibility. As I truly recognize that God has purposefully placed these three souls under my care and direction. It is a chapter of great responsibility and joy that consumes my every moment, as I attempt to approach each line through His guidance. I know that there is nothing, apart from their father, that is more important than these remarkable blessings within my life. Each of them beautifully created by Him with unique gifts crafted with expectations and purpose. As a parent, we are tasked with the calling and responsibility of equipping and preparing them to live a life for Him—A life that is composed of His story, filled with His purpose. I have realized and recognized that the joy found within this chapter comes from pointing them to Him. We are called to bring them up in the training and instruction of the Lord, as exclaimed in Ephesians 6:4.

The pages of this journey continue to turn at an incredible pace as I watch three of the most amazing gifts God would bless my life with change and grow with each turn. As I watch the words be scripted within each of their individual chapters, I am overwhelmed by the *joy* they bring within my pages— pages filled with such triumph yet challenge. I am continuing to learn this is by far the most difficult yet rewarding calling placed on my life. The fact that God has chosen me to guide, mold, and direct them each toward Him within their journey is an overwhelming responsibility. They are, along with their amazing father, the ministry that I have been called within this chapter. I am called to love them in a way that brings glory to

Him. Fifteen years within this journey, I set my eyes upon Him as I strive to live a life as described in Proverbs 31:25–31:

"She is clothed with strength and dignity; she can laugh at the days to come. She speaks with wisdom, and faithful instruction is on her tongue. She watches over the affairs of her household and does not eat the bread of idleness. Her children arise and call her blessed; her husband also, and he praises her: "Many women do noble things, but you surpass them all." Charm is deceptive, and beauty is fleeting; but a woman who fears the Lord is to be praised. Honor her for all that her hands have done, and let her works bring her praise at the city gate."

This being one of the greatest callings on my life, I recognize the *joy* within this blessing but also realize the significance.

As Proverbs 22:6 teaches, the path that we as parents direct them upon will be one in which they will remain.

As the years have quickly passed within this chapter, I have had the privilege of watching God answer the most important prayer that I have prayed over each of my children. All three of my children have come to know the saving knowledge of Jesus Christ, accepting and professing Him as their personal Lord and Savior. I praise God for their salvation, and I rejoice knowing that they have found their one true source of everlasting joy in Him. I am continuing to pray for each of them to grow in their relationship becoming mighty warriors for Him. Attempting to always point them in His direction, I am filled with such pride as I watch them mature in their walk. Recognizing the love of a mother and the joy encompassed in that title, I cannot help but be brought to my knees. I think about the depth of which I love my three children and then begin to realize that does not even compare to the depth of love our Heavenly Father bestows upon each of His children. I cannot even fully understand that reality, but I am consumed by the recognition of such an undeserving *joy!*

Chapter 8

SUPPORT

Throughout my journey, a consistent blessing of joy has been delicately woven upon each page. It is only as I turn back the pages within my journey have I truly recognized the powerful joy found within the blessing of support. God has and continues to intrinsically weave the most amazing support network among each page. This network being so vital to the turn of each page within my chapters but often missed as I focused on my quest of perfection driven by my battle of fear.

God has purposefully written within my story a network of people who pour real joy into my life. Each loving me with an authentic love resembling the love described in 1 Corinthians 13:4–7, "Love is patient, love is kind. It does not envy, it does not boast, it is not proud. It does not dishonor others, it is not self-seeking, it is not easily angered, it keeps no record of wrongs. Love does not delight in evil but rejoices with the truth. It always protects, always trusts, always hopes, always perseveres." This love recognized in my older age as an undeserving gift and realized as an incredible source of my joy.

I recognized early that God had chosen to bless me with a family that loved unconditionally and supported me sacrificially. A family that loved me much more than I deserved, filling my life with fear-crushing joy. As the pages continue to turn, and the years add on to my life, I am learning to recognize the power within this blessing of joy. This power truly able to crush fear and eliminate any earthly desire of perfection, setting my eyes on my true source of fulfilling JOY and purpose.

This support network, that God had so intrinsically woven into each chapter, was not solely comprised of pure-blooded family. God had chosen my family, but he had so beautifully led me in choosing my friends. A network of such beautiful souls scattered throughout the pages of my journey, writing lasting impact upon the pages and within my heart. I so often discuss with my three children the importance of choosing their friends, encouraging them to surround their lives with people who point them to Him. As a growing teenager, I had been taught that my life would either lead people closer to Him or lead them in the other direction. As Proverbs 13:20 teaches, "He who walks with the wise grows wise, but a companion of fools suffers harm."

The importance and support of these friends have and continue to be instrumental within my journey. Each providing strength, counsel, and encouragement as we strive to live a life for Him. Proverbs 27:17 speaks of that truth stating, "As iron sharpens iron, so one person sharpens another." Recognizing that our attempt of this life is filled with imperfections, but true authentic friendship refreshes the soul as described in Proverbs 27:9. Within this authenticity, we realize the need we have for each other, His guidance, and the joy that need provides.

This need also challenges me to strive each day to become more like Him in my approach to each acquaintance. So often we miss this incredible calling within our lives to simply love others as He has loved us. We consistently choose to view each person within our path with our own judgment of worth in our approach to serve or dismiss. A terribly frightening misconception and understanding of human nature defined by a self-entitled social culture. We all deserve nothing based on our own merit, but yet He chose to give us everything. Why then is it so hard for us to view others through His own lens instead of through our own distorted view?

I think we simply become distracted by what this world defines as worth versus what the Creator of this world deems as worthy, just as we seek our own personal desired happiness instead of seeking ultimate joy found within Him. God said in Genesis 1:26, "Let us make mankind in our image, in our likeness, so that they may rule over the fish in the sea and the birds in the sky, over the livestock and all the wild animals and over all the creatures that move along the ground."

According to this scripture, we are made in God's image and are set apart to resemble our incredible Creator. Each of us is designed uniquely and perfectly by our Creator to have dominion over all other animals. We were each created to have fellowship with our heavenly Father and with others. We are challenged to disregard our own definition of worth and seek His lens of love. We need each other as we flip the pages of our individual lives and are called to love one another through encouragement. In the New American Standard Bible, First Thessalonians 5:11 states, "Therefore encourage one another and build up one another, just as you also are doing." Putting our differences aside and approaching each other through His lens creates a beautiful network within each page of one's chapter. As communicated in John 13:34, we are called to love one another as He has loved us. When we choose to realize the importance of this calling to love one another, we then begin to recognize the beautiful joy within the network. As I quickly turn the pages of each chapter, I am amazed at the people within my journey who do this so well. Each creating a contagious ripple of positivity and encouragement that radiates His love to all within the light. I am thankful for each of these incredible people God has placed within my life, and I am challenged by their obedience within the joy. I am challenged to become more like them in their approach to loving and serving others, ultimately becoming more like my Creator who has called us into action. An action exemplified beautifully by friends described in the following verses:

"Some men came carrying a paralyzed man on a mat and tried to take him into the house to lay him before Jesus. When they could not find a way to do this because of the crowd, they went up on the roof and lowered him on his mat through the tiles into the middle of the crowd, right in front of Jesus." (Luke 5:18–19)

We are called to be the type of friend that would be willing to tear through a roof to get someone to Jesus. Also, we are challenged to surround ourselves with friends that would be willing to tear through a roof on our behalf. We are called to point others toward Christ and be willing to do whatever it takes to keep each other right in front of Jesus. This challenge creates a great need within us. A need that is filled intentionally by our heavenly Father, but a need that is up to each one of us to recognize. A need, once recognized, that requires our own effort and action to fully comprehend the value of its support.

As I flip through the pages of this chapter, I am overwhelmed by the beauty within each example of His scripted support. It was so evident within each triumph of success, and it covered every fiber of failure. This indescribable and sometimes unrecognizable support enveloped every turn of my page. The joy within the pages of this chapter are endless, and I continue to recognize the beauty found within that joy with each turn of a day.

In life, we often attempt to surround ourselves with people that make us feel comfortable or worthy through a false sense of continuous praise. If we are honest, this is exactly what we often desire. We look for a continuous pat on the back, an empty praise of positivity, or simply an acknowledgement of agreement and confirmation. This misleading desire is often sought regardless of its validity. Once again, allowing the temporary desires of our selfish pursuit of acceptance to be defined by others definition of our worth rather than allowing God alone to define our identity and self-worth. Throughout my life, I have sometimes found myself within relationships defined by this temporary attempt of social acceptance and even worse—admiration. God has called us to so much more than this fleeting world's definition of worth.

We often lose ourselves in a twisted attempt of gaining approval within a falsely defining society. A society that attempts to define and label one's self-worth by their social status or club membership. Within early adulthood, I began to realize my misguided attempt of creating self-seeking support. I recognized the desperate need within my heart to surround myself with people that pointed me only toward my Savior. These people confirming and encouraging within me a resounding truth—my worth is defined only by Him. Our society attempts to misdirect each of us with a disturbing and dangerous pursuit of lies. Lies that consume so many with behavior, effort, time, and resources. All of which is wasted in an attempt of being defined or labeled by a fallen society. These labels fading with time and worthless within eternity.

Our true worth defined by Him is what should drive all of our behavior, effort, time, and resources. A worth that is immeasurable when operating according to His calling on one's life. A calling that my friends take with great responsibility. True friendship is a calling that encourages and challenges me through genuine authenticity. The people that fill the lines within this chapter are an indescribably beautiful example of what He calls us to within genuine friendship. I am truly overwhelmed as I think through the names scripted across my pages of incredible friendships. A life full of relationships that characterize the true meaning of support. As I think about the people scripted upon every page of my chapter, I am reminded of their importance. These friends view me and others through His lens, and they encourage me to do the same. Just like my parents in early childhood and coaches within my early years of competition, these friends hold me accountable to being the best version of myself. A version that reflects Him. This support and love creating expectations within our relationship. Expectations created by our shared Savior but exemplified through their amazing admirable lives.

Living a life that encompasses an unconditional attempt of support without barriers or limitations. Each of us together striving to live a life that radiates His beauty. This support encouraging and challenging each other that this reflection should be evident within our marriages, friendships, parenting, and everywhere. It should consume our language and eliminate the dangerous judgment found within our mistaken gossip. A support that equips each other with His power that will defeat and conquer all that this quick life may throw our way. This support defined by Him, not the society around us. It is vitally important to purposely surround ourselves with these powerful types of friendships. It is one's choice on whom to place within their pages. A choice that can have an immeasurable impact on so many chapters within a life. An impact that will either point us closer to Him or pull us farther away from Him.

This is an eye-opening revelation as you think of the incredible opportunity or consequences that these choices will have on our lives. As I continuously discuss with my children the importance that lies within their decision of whom they choose to surround themselves with inside their own pages, I am reminded of the importance of this choice within my own life. This choice having incredible impact and influence as we all strive to live a life that points others toward Him. This is a choice that remains vitally important at any age as I am encouraged daily by beautiful friendships that encourage and challenge me through accountability. This genuine and authentic friendship is not one of rose-colored glasses but true transparency and grace.

As I look around, I need no help in recognizing the extreme joy produced by the many people God has orchestrated as my support. This chapter exudes genuine joy as these remarkable people love and lead me in the direction of Him. A chapter slammed full of individuals intentionally placed within the lines of my life. Each line scripted with the purpose of creating a lasting joy found in their words. I am fully aware that I do not deserve the genuine joy produced by the friendship of these beautiful souls I call my friends, but I will be forever grateful— grateful to my heavenly Father for placing such souls upon the pages of this chapter and for helping me recognize my desperate need for their support.

These friends of mine would, in fact, tear through any roof to get me closer to my Savior, and I would without hesitation destroy any roof or obstacle to get them closer to Him. I am so thankful for a genuine joy producing support that is character-ized by the encouragement found from being united in His love as described in the following passage:

"Therefore if you have any encouragement from being united with Christ, if any comfort from his love, if any common sharing in the Spirit, if any tenderness and compassion, then make my joy complete by being like-minded, having the same love, being one in spirit and of one mind. Do nothing out of selfish ambition or vain conceit. Rather, in humility value others above yourselves, not looking to your own interests but each of you to the interests of the others. In your relationships with one another, have the same mindset as Christ Jesus: Who, being in very nature God, did not consider equality with God something to be used to his own advantage; rather, he made himself nothing by taking the very nature of a servant, being made in human likeness. And being found in appearance as a man, he humbled himself by becoming obedient to death—even death on a cross! Therefore God exalted him to the highest place and gave him the name that is above every name, that at the name of Jesus every knee should bow, in heaven and on earth and under the earth, and every tongue acknowledge that Jesus Christ is Lord, to the glory of God the Father." (Philippians 2: 1–11)

Throughout each chapter of my life, there are so many names scripted throughout my journey that provide such immeasurable support. My life was and continues to be filled with a recognition and celebration of such amazing people within my journey. These people forming the most beautiful and inspiring source of blessing found within their support. A blessing of joy through their love as described in Philemon 1:7, "Your love has given me great joy and encouragement, because you, brother, have refreshed the hearts of the Lord's people." My heart continues to be refreshed through the amazing people that God has so beautifully orchestrated as my support.

Chapter 9

IDENTITY

In my early chapters of childhood, competition, and career, I would pursue the impossible quest of perfection. This false perception of perfection defined the very identity of each page within my journey. My inner drive to compete not only propelled an aggressive career in athletics but an impossible attempt of achieving the best of each title within my identity. Only soon I would realize as the pages quickly fall, I was not being called to be the very best within every title but rather to become the very best version of His title for me. A title that would be realized after many unimportant banners would be placed across my chapter. These banners full of momentary selfish glory that would fade with the flip of a page and propel me into another quest for accomplishment.

The upstairs playroom within my childhood home had quickly been turned into what one may call a Museum of Titles as it would house the accolades of my very successful quest of perfection within my identity. Each trophy, medal, ranking, crown, and title added to my increasingly growing false sense of entitlement. Looking in from the outside, it seemed within my life that everything I touched would turn to gold or silver resulting in a new title added to my banner.

As a small child, I remember being quite conscientious of my muscular build. My mother would constantly encourage me by discussing all the positives involving each aspect of my life, but I was not buying what she was selling in regards to an upcoming pageant.

She was clearly just trying to make me feel better about my athletic build. I would take some comfort in her words, but I could not believe she was making me be in a pageant. My cousins both entered into the local county pageant, so I guess my mother thought I should be involved as well. I was literally wearing a bright pink dress with the skirt portion resembling the tutu of a Halloween costume! One thing did spark my interest, and that was this pageant was at the very core of its insanity—a competition. So when thrust into any type of competition, I was going to give it my best shot. Uncomfortable with the look of my legs in this short pink tutu, my white rolled-down lace socks and my white high heels, I stepped out onto that stage with one purpose and stepped off with my first crown. Little Miss Pike County was scripted across my banner. A trophy taller than me stood by my side, and a silver bejeweled crown was placed on my head. My mom was proud, and I was satisfied with the win. Little Miss Pike County became the first of many titles written across the pages of my identity.

Quickly discovering my athletic legs were much better suited for a court of some sort, the success would follow. By the time I was twelve, I had achieved the number one junior ranking within the state, launching me into the national junior tour, traveling the country with the top junior players competing and winning at the highest level. I would remain a top-ranked junior for the next six years lending me the opportunities of a lifetime. Completely captivated by the competition and the drive to win, it would take me across the United States and Europe scripting titles across my ever growing banner of identity. Upon graduating high school, I was awarded the prestigious Don Souder Award. This award was presented to the most outstanding senior athlete in the Mississippi Academy of Private Schools, and overwhelmed with this honor, I would look to my next challenge. This challenge would begin as I embarked upon my collegiate career. This achievement being the overall goal of my athletic career and ended at the college of my choice.

With a banner full of athletic accolades, my identity longed for more than just sports titles and success. I was content with nothing less than every aspect of my life, finding the utmost outward perfection. Excelling at academics throughout my high school and collegiate career was another banner that was quickly scripted through this journey. Titles and awards mounting, I also needed to obtain a well-rounded young life lending to an impressive resume, throwing myself into every leadership role that was available and becoming elected to roles of prestige. I seemed to be living the small-town dream. Titles added to an identity driven by perfection and an intense effort to avoid any resemblance of failure. Looking back, my quest in conquering academic perfection laddered up to the planned identity that I had already determined for my future. As I entered into a pre-med major with a transcript of perfection at the University of Mississippi, the challenge of obtaining academic perfection would be agonizing as a student athlete. A challenge that would only push me to work harder, seeking yet another scripted title to add to my banner of success. That predetermined identity that I had already picked for myself would afford me the inability to become content with the leadership roles and accolades of an impressive high school career. The small-town homecoming queen would need to achieve much more to fill her collegiate resume with admirable accolades to assist in her overall plan of her ultimate identity.

Hundreds gathered around the steps of the student union at the University of Mississippi as we awaited the results. "And the 2000 Miss Ole Miss is…Missy Brewer!" Surrounded by screams, hugs, tears, and laughter, I could not believe my ears. I had just been elected to the most insane title of my life! Scripted across the banner of this chapter was a title I would have never dreamed a possibility. Elected by the student body, this award would be one that meant the most as it represented the incredible hard work that had been poured into these last four years of my collegiate career. That night, when the celebration had ended and I was back in my quiet room at my sorority house, I would find myself staring at the flyer containing my picture and all my collegiate accolades. Proud within the moment, I was quickly reminded of what this newly-elected title would do for my pre-planned identity for my future. Never content within the moment of success and always looking forward to the next win, I would finish this year with a mission.

As the president of the Pre-Med Honor Society, I was involved with the Career Day at Ole Miss. I had already planned my professional future and had chosen my identity within a career following medical school but was excited to be involved with this process. Working with several pharmaceutical companies, I got to know the recruiters from the highly sought-after Fortune 500 Companies. As the week concluded, I would find myself interviewing with several of them just to appease their request.

We raced to the university post office located within the student union as we all knew what would be waiting with the turn of our keys. Each of us had worked so hard for four years leading up to this moment! Endless all-night study groups, endless hours within the library, endless hours upon the court, and endless volunteer and leadership hours all leading up to this very moment. This small group of friends had survived the challenge, completing our challenging pre-med majors, and finishing with honors. We were excited to open our acceptance letters to the University of Mississippi Medical School. As I ripped the letter open, I began to read the following, "Missy, we are sorry to inform you that…" I don't remember much more of the generic letter of rejection. Slowly removing myself from the crowded student union with eyes full of rejection tears, I was having trouble processing the news of what I interpreted as failure. *This must be wrong*, my mind would think as I walked what felt like miles back to my sorority house that afternoon. My arrogant and entitled mind truly could not process failure. That flyer with my picture and all the accolades flashed through my head along with a near-perfect transcript. With tears flowing heavily, I am now hysterical in a rare moment of defeat. The pages of my collegiate life would be over in what seemed like a flash. I felt as if I was facing the biggest loss within my journey. I replayed in my mind all of the hard work that had gone into all of those awarded titles, the elected ones, and the achieved ones. All of these a misrepresentation of an apparent triumph. *What did they want?* I thought to myself! *What did I miss?* Looking back at this moment, I am overcome with a heart wrenching reality! It was not about what they wanted or what I had wanted and so perfectly orchestrated—it was about what He wanted and had planned for my life. A plan directing me to the only true identity within myself—my identity in Christ. A plan that I had not even sought so blinded by my arrogant attempt at perfection and personal desire. I would learn and continue to learn that no title ever achieved or earned within this lifetime would ever compare to the title we would find in Him.

Looking back at this chapter, I am overwhelmed with the provision of my Savior throughout such a selfish pursuit of my plan. Reminded within the words of Jeremiah 1:5, "He knew me before He formed me in the womb and had already set me apart for His plan within my journey," leading and teaching me through each challenge or battle and with each success and failure. He was molding me into a daughter that He could use for His glory, placing His crown of adoption upon my life. He had provided such incredible opportunity within the every page of my journey, scripting beautiful blessing and *joy* within a planned future for my life that is so much greater in comparison to the letters within the title MD. As I was busy appeasing the pharmaceutical companies with an interview, God was scripting the words of an amazing career and future. A letter would introduce me to His plans in the form of an incredible offer from one of those Fortune 500 Companies. That offer allowed me to choose my location and to secure a career with a company that, eighteen years later, I am still blessed to be a part of. A career that would place me in the same city as my future husband leading to a wedding the following year. A career that would afford me the ability to dive into a challenging medical career dedicated to bettering patients' lives. A career that would allow me to find success personally and professionally as it would support me through three pregnancies. I am broken each time I think through the reality of how God knew the importance of motherhood within my identity before I even knew I would have children. He was guiding and providing a career that would afford me the opportunity to do both and be present within the every page of their growing life. A career that, as a working mother, supports me in maintaining a healthy work family balance with the recognition and support of the fact my family will always be my priority. His plan is more perfect than anything that I could have ever imagined for my life. My banners I excitedly traded for the one crown that I proudly wear upon my head as a daughter of the one true King. My life redirected from a life of perfection to a life guided by His perfect plan. A life guided by the ultimate *perfecter*. One of my favorite verses is found in Jeremiah 29:11. This verse provides the underlying drive inside this chapter as God reminds me of His ultimate control of an unimaginable future in Him.

> "For I know the plans I have for you, declares
> the Lord, plans to prosper you and not to harm
> you, plans to give you hope and a future."

The *joy* is not found in the identity of the title but the impact you make within it. Each title and accolade representing the One who blessed you with the ability and guidance to achieve it. All was laddering up to a beautifully scripted identity and future that our heavenly Father orchestrates on our behalf. A perfectly orchestrated plan pointing toward the one and only source of our identity found only in Christ. I find my identity in Him alone.

Chapter 10

CALLING

"For I live in eager expectation and hope that I will never do anything that causes me shame, but that I will always be bold for Christ, whether I live or die. For to me, living is for Christ, and dying is even better." (Philippians 1:20–21 New Living Translation)

As I began to grow in the realization of my identity within Christ, I began to try and understand his calling upon my life. Throughout so many chapters of my life, I was misguided by so many misleading distractions within this journey. During childhood, I was dreaming of success but limited by fear. During adolescence, I was lost within a checklist and a pursuit of titles and even in early adulthood struggling to understand His calling upon my life. As I sought Him in my understanding and gained a genuine recognition of the *joy* within my journey, He began to unveil an incredible calling to ministry.

"Was God calling me into ministry?" I would ask myself as I sought His guidance. And the answer was quite resounding— *yes*! Within that answer, I understood that every child of God was called into ministry. It is our responsibility to recognize the call within our individual ministry. I had in my attempt of forming my own self-limiting definition of ministry limited the very calling He had already placed upon my life. I tried to limit His calling to one specific title and struggled with the discernment of that calling. Through this struggle, He spoke such truth within my life showing me the joy within a personal ministry already in motion. A calling to pursue with every fiber of my being—one that he had already scripted in advance: a plan far greater than any dream or selfish pursuit that I could have imagined. As followers of Christ, we are all called into His ministry! Each of these ministries may look different, but all should reflect a common purpose! That purpose should focus on bringing honor and glory to our Savior through every aspect of our life! I would and continue to embark on a newly-defined journey embracing each ministry. A call to come together with other believers partnering together through Christ to accomplish our overall purpose! A partnership that will encourage each other through the study of God's Word, prayer, and sharing of our testimonies. A call mentioned and defined in Chapter 1 as He delivers the Great Commission found in the following verses of Matthew 28:

> "All authority in heaven and on earth has been given to me. Therefore go and make disciples of all nations, baptizing them in the name of the Father and of the Son and of the Holy Spirit, and teaching them to obey everything I have commanded you. And surely I am with you always, to the very end of the age."

I have learned and continue to learn that the joy lies in the true recognition of each ministry that God has called me into and already placed me within. And in that realization is a call to hold myself and others accountable. He has shown me within my quest for titles the important titles that He had already scripted across my personal banner: child of God, wife, mother, daughter, sister, and friend. Within each of these titles, He has already provided the definition of my calling. Are we giving Him complete honor and glory through our ministry each day? As I recognize the importance of each ministry, I am encouraged by the guidance His Word provides within each calling.

First and foremost, I am called to be a *child* of God. Identifying that my true identity lies within Him, I have recognized the real joy is found within that relationship. That relationship is calling me to my greatest responsibility of my faith.

> "For I live in eager expectation and hope that I will never do anything that causes me shame, but that I will always be bold for Christ, whether I live or die. For to me, living is for Christ, and dying is even better." (Philippians 1:20–21 New Living Translation)

As a *wife*, I am striving to exemplify the description within Proverbs 31:

"She is clothed with strength and dignity, and she laughs with no fear of the future. When she speaks, her words are wise, and kindness is the rule when she gives instructions. She carefully watches all that goes on in her household and does not have to bear the consequences of laziness. Her children stand and bless her. Her husband praises her. There are many virtuous and capable women in the world, but you surpass them all!" (Proverbs 31:25–29 New Living Translation)

I am a *mother* of three precious gifts. These gifts each holding an incredible responsibility as I am called to lead them toward Him, finding challenge and encouragement from the New Living Translation of Proverbs 22:6, "Teach your children to choose the right path, and when they are older, they will remain upon it."

As a *daughter*, I am called to much more than simply learning from my parents. We learn early within the commandments the importance of obedience and honor. The importance explained in Ephesians 6:1–3:

> "Obey your parents because you belong to the Lord, for this is the right thing to do. Honor your father and mother. This is the first of the Ten Commandments that ends with a promise. And this is the promise: If you honor your father and mother, you will live a long life, full of blessing." (Ephesians 6:1–3 New Living Translation)

Each of us are called into different career paths; but all of us, as Christians, are called to make an impact within that *career*, recognizing the opportunity in which we have been placed. He does not make mistakes in scripting our plans, so I have learned and continue to learn that I am placed within each page with specific purpose. Many times, upon looking back, I have missed opportunities to share Christ's love due to the distractions of my earthly responsibility. I continuously am misdirected by a selfish and prideful pursuit of personal achievement only to be quickly reminded it is never intended to be about me.

Recognizing within each failure, the urgent commitment to the challenge as described within 1 Corinthians 15:58, "Therefore, my dear brothers and sisters, stand firm. Let nothing move you. Always give yourselves fully to the work of the Lord, because you know that your labor in the Lord is not in vain."

As a *sister* and *friend*, I have been blessed beyond description through love. Proverbs 17:17 says a friend loves at all time; and from a young sister who assisted in defeating fear to a lifetime friend of authenticity—I have learned the definition of loving through this ministry. A love that is defining our ultimate identity in Him as beautifully scripted in John 13:34–35, "Love one another. As I have loved you, so you must love one another. By this everyone will know that you are my disciples, if you love one another." I continue to learn as I seek a life defined by His glory within each area of ministry but recognize this calling holds great responsibility. The two verses below reiterate this call upon my life:

"So, whether you eat or drink, or whatever you do, do all to the glory of God." (1 Corinthians 10:31 English Standard Version)

"Love the Lord your God with all your heart and with all your soul and with all your strength. These commandments that I give you today are to be on your hearts. Impress them on your children. Talk about them when you sit at home and when you walk along the road, when you lie down and when you get up. Tie them as symbols on your hands and bind them on your foreheads." (Deuteronomy 6:5–8)

Each of us must take individual ownership within our calling; but also commit to holding ourselves and others accountable in this journey—a call to empower each other within ministry through prayer and encouragement. Partnership that spreads across generations, leading each to learn from each other and grow in Christ! I find comfort in resting in God's Word, and my purpose in life is fulfilled through Him! My prayer is that my life and my ministry will bring Him great honor and glory! I am excited as with each flip of the page within my journey, God continues to call me to more within His plan. His titles are defining the direction of each new chapter; and with each word scripted, growing me closer in my relationship with Him.

Chapter 11

SALVATION

Each and every chapter within my journey of life ladders up to the most important chapter that defines my identity, my purpose, and my ultimate source of *joy*. Salvation, for those who choose to accept it, defines the very words upon each page within our story. Some find it early in life, some in the middle of their journey, and some as the last page is being turned; but for all who find it are victorious.

One of the greatest blessings of my life is the fact that from the time of my conception, I had been within the church. While yet in the womb, the hope of my salvation was being prayed. The mother that God had chosen for me was an obedient warrior, taking her responsibility with an intensity that was unmatched. There are not words that could accurately describe the power of a praying mother as she was and is a faithful warrior on my behalf. From as early as I can remember, my parents led in a way that pointed others to Him, loving and serving our Lord with a consistent and unwavering mission. Each leading and teaching within our church and community made an impact on many, but the depth of that impact was no greater than within myself as I watched and learned from not just their words but their admirable actions. They lived and continue to live their life with a purpose, a purpose guided by the hope of their salvation.

One night after Wednesday night church, my mother's prayer for me was answered as I prayed to accept Christ as my personal Lord and Savior. Sitting on the side of my bed with both my parents, I made the biggest and best decision of my life. With child-like faith at seven years old, I knew I needed Jesus and deeply desired the hope of an eternity with Him. I knew with the depth of understanding of a child that I needed forgiveness, and I can remember the indescribable sense of joy and peace that flooded my small heart as I received the Holy Spirit that Wednesday night. This began the most incredible journey one is called to within their life. A journey that only begins within this chapter and gloriously extends into eternity.

That night as I prayed, I took the first step into the journey of what true salvation entails. As Romans 10:9–10 states:

> "If you declare with your mouth, "Jesus is Lord," and believe in your heart that God raised him from the dead, you will be saved. For it is with your heart that you believe and are justified, and it is with your mouth that you profess your faith and are saved."

And as my journey continues, God is filling my pages with more than I could ever imagine! Growing up within the household I did, it was not an option that we would attend church. It was understood within our family that it was our number one priority, and not until much later in the maturity within my faith would I understand just how important the presence within God's house would become within my life.

As a teenager, walking within my faith at times would appear more like a roller-coaster ride rather than a walk. As I struggled with understanding the calling upon my life through my salvation, I would fail miserably at my attempt to balance both my worlds. A perfectionist at heart, I had convinced myself that my salvation was calling me to perfect an internal checklist that was evident for all to see the success. Religion had consumed my entire outlook on life.

- ☐ NO cussing
- ☐ NO lying
- ☐ NO cheating
- ☐ NO using God's name in vain
- ☐ NO drinking
- ☐ NO sex

- ☐ Read Bible
- ☐ Pray
- ☐ Church
- ☐ Lead Bible Study
- ☐ Devotional
- ☐ Missions

As I grew closer to Christ, my list would increase and the torment of perfection would consume. As a leader within my youth group, I would struggle with the outside pressures of the world, ultimately causing me to erase the checks off certain blocks within my list as I would fail consistently in my achievement of perfection. I was allowing my personal desire of perfection and responsibility to drive my non-existent growth instead of allowing the Holy Spirit to consume and lead my growth.

The Holy Spirit within me constantly and consistently protected me through conviction and guidance. Always redirecting me to Him, I would often miss the source of guidance due to the blinding influence of my list. I convinced myself that if I could keep my checklist of perfection in check that I was walking in the direction He called. It is amazing as I look back upon the teenage years of my life as to how faithful God was amid my stupidity and selfish pursuit of a checklist. In Deuteronomy 31:8, it states, "The Lord himself goes before you and will be with you; he will never leave you nor forsake you. Do not be afraid; do not be discouraged."

My life is such an incredible example of His ever-present love for His children. How could I not see that I was *never* going to be able to obtain a perfect Christian checklist and perfection was not what my salvation had called me to within my life? My mistakes, my failures, my bad decisions, and my human error were what brought me to the side of my bed as a seven-year-old child and what my Savior had already redeemed. As I grew in age, my list only intensified in early adulthood, but God was not or never had been calling me to perfection! He had called me to redemption and taken that burden from me. Perfection was and is impossible, and in my misguided pursuit of what I thought was defined as a *good Christian*, I had missed the *joy* within my very salvation. God had not been calling me to perfection within a religious checklist, and religion was not what He desired for my life. He desperately was seeking an intimate growing relationship filled with redemption and grace. I had become stuck within my salvation, comfortable and complacent with knowing the hope of eternity but living in a manner under my own control—stagnant in my relationship. Wrestling with the Holy Spirit, I sought Him desperately seeking an understanding of what He was telling me. Even doubting my salvation and confused by the conviction, God took me to my knees one night in my small rental house, and I let go. I mean, I really let go. I gave it all to Him for the first time in as long as I could remember. He was calling me to so much more within my salvation—*yes*! His plans were becoming so clear within a growing relationship with Him. More than twenty years following my first step into my salvation, I was completely overcome with His peace and *joy*! I had been struggling with what He was calling me to do, and in that moment, I realized He was simply calling me to return to Him and allow Him to use me through His guidance and desiring for me to grow more intimately in love with Him as each page of my journey was turned. He was calling me to hand over my entire life, my checklist, my religion, and commit to the most mind-blowing relationship that one could imagine. I was and am no longer burdened by a checklist but rather guided by His Word.

For years, I had missed it. I had thrown myself into so many things that I thought God wanted me to do, so I could check them off the list—all things that are good at their core and things that become fruitful within a healthy-growing relationship with Him. The items of my teenage and young adult Christian checklist would quickly turn from obligations of my faith to healthy fruitful byproducts of my walk with Him. As an adult Sunday school teacher, I walked the aisle within the same church that I had walked as a seven-year-old girl. Putting the stake in the ground and my prideful list in the garbage, I made a public profession of faith and was baptized again. I knew that I had been saved at seven. My salvation was evident within my life as the Holy Spirit had guided my entire life and provided the most beautiful provision over my life through so many turbulent years! I also knew that the Holy Spirit was calling me to make that decision public; and not remembering my first baptism, I wanted to remember professing my faith through believer's baptism. Some may say an unnecessary step, but I would say an obedient step that has transformed my walk with my Savior.

So many settle with the hope found in their mere acceptance of our Savior and never truly come to the full realization of what He is calling us to within our salvation. It is so much more than a decision. It is a real relationship transforming a lifestyle guided and directed by His light. The decision is just the first step of salvation. The *joy* is found in the personal growing relationship with Him. I am so incredibly thankful for the Holy Spirit's aggressive calling on my soul to seek so much more in Him through a growing and thriving relationship. A relationship that encourages and equips each word written across every page of my undeserving life. A relationship that has allowed and continues to allow the discovery and recognition of so much immeasurable *joy* intertwined perfectly within each chapter of my life. It is and always has been right in front of me but is only fully recognized through His lens.

God, I will never understand why you love me the way that you do and that you choose to use me, but I will never stop seeking you and your amazing plan, following without question, and striving to become more like you until the last period is placed within my story. Upon that placement, I can only imagine the magnificent moment of when my story turns to an endless celebration of eternal worship and when I am standing face-to-face with the *One* who gave me life, salvation, purpose, hope, comfort, healing, redemption, grace, and joy—the *One* who gave me everything!

Until then, I cling tightly to the *joy* I have found in Christ!

Chapter 12

HEAVEN

I often think about the glorious day of when I will see my Savior face-to-face and try to imagine its magnificence. Within those thoughts, I am often reminded of an impactful moment found within the pages of my journey. A moment that was filled with such incredible beauty. Looking back into the conversations with my young daughter, I can't recall the exact details spoken within the amazing discussions, but I will never forget the impact of the joy found within each discussion.

One late night as I attempted to get my young daughter to bed, she embarked on a conversation that would etch an unforgettable moment within the pages of both our lives. She began to talk about someone with incredible excitement. She talked about her beauty and bright-colored wings. My young daughter explained in so many words the gigantic size of her wings and talked about how bright the light was within this description.

I listened perplexed but fascinated as my young daughter continued her description of what in detail appeared to be some sort of magnificent angel. I don't remember all the details of her descriptions but do remember my amazement as she explained that it was Too Too. She continued her amazing explanation with a sparkling glimmer of awe-inspiring excitement in her big blue eyes. As her bright eyes spoke more than her words, swallowing difficulty, tears began to fill my eyes.

In my daughter's room, there was a pink-framed picture of my beautiful grandmother, Too Too. In this picture, my grandmother was holding my then week-old daughter Carlyle. This picture had been taken less than two months prior to my grandmother's passing years earlier. Within this favorite picture of mine, she was looking with admiration at her newest great-granddaughter. I was taken aback to that moment within my living room as my grandmother had sat gleaming with pride as she held her newest great-granddaughter. We talked about just how grand we thought she was and discussed how incredibly grand our excitement was for my grandmothers ninetieth birthday. We had laughed at the adventures of our past, and she talked about the hope within the adventures of her newest great-grandchild. She beamed with radiance when talking about her many grandchildren and great-grandchildren and prayed for each of their hopeful futures with intensity. I remember within that moment as she sat holding my daughter so proudly, I was the one filled with such pride as I admired the love of my grandmother. I remember how thankful I was within that very moment.

My young daughter would blow my mind as she would continue to explain that my grandmother was indeed whom she was talking about within her radiant description. She would describe various things that occurred within her experience. I wish I could remember every one of her exact words as she described these incredible details. But as I recall at that moment, she would continue to explain in vivid details that she looked different, young, beautiful, and with huge bright wings. I must have at that moment been wiping the tears, and taking a deep breath trying to control my composure. It was difficult to try and understand the conversation. Carlyle had no memory of my grandmother as she was not even two months old when she passed. So how was this explainable?

We had not discussed my grandmother in quite some time and only rarely in the past in reference to whom that was in the framed picture sitting on her shelf. I began to ask more questions in my attempt to understand. She would describe that she would see her in apparent dreams or visions. She continued to tell me of the things she had seen and the magnificent description of a youthful, radiant version of my grandmother.

After discussing this mind-blowing and inspiring vision of beauty with my young daughter, I can remember being completely overwhelmed with intense emotion. Filled with unexplainable elation, I tried to process the conversation I had just had with my precious daughter. None of it making sense, yet creating an explosion of joy throughout my being. Following that conversation, I would find myself mesmerized within the details. I would also find myself longing for one last glimpse into my grandmother's eyes. I desired one more conversation filled with one more sound of her laughter. I needed one more handwritten note of her encouragement. I simply longed for one more moment within a page of her beautifully scripted life. I knew the reality within my request, but I also knew of the miraculous power of my God. I began to call out to my heavenly Father in a desperate understanding of my daughter's apparent vision or dream. She was too young to even understand or imagine the beauty that she described in such detail, so I found myself questioning the reality of this possibility.

I found myself in that moment amid my tears, praying for one more moment with my grandmother. As strange as that may seem, I literally wept in prayer asking Him to allow me to see the beauty that my daughter had described, and I longed for a glimpse within the magnificent vision of my heavenly grandmother. I missed her so deeply. Were the words from my daughter a gift from my heavenly Father to help me heal within my grief or had she truly experienced an unexplainable glimpse within the glory of heaven. I fell asleep that night hoping for a miraculous dream filled with her presence. As I woke the next morning, I had in fact not been given the request of my longing heart. I would not ever be granted the answer to my audacious request, but through His Word would be reminded of the day it will be fulfilled in full. As I live a life of eager expectation, I am frequently reminded of her beauty through the memory of her extraordinarily impactful life. My daughter would continue to discuss on multiple occasions different experiences of seeing my grandmother. Each providing unexplainable beauty, comfort, and joy within their description.

My grandmother's favorite verse found in Psalm 30:5 described that weeping may last through the night, but joy comes with the morning. I knew that she had found her joy the moment her last chapter concluded in her earthly journey. My grandmother had lived a beautiful and impactful life, a life characterized by love. Her life exuded His love; a love that conquered all things. Her love resembling the intricately detailed beauty described within the dreams of Carlyle. Dreams describing the magnificent radiance of such majestic wings. Wings that were described with such rich moving color, similar to the most beautiful butterfly imagined. This love exemplified all that we are called to be upon our walk through this journey. She realized and recognized the JOY within each of her chapters.

Each chapter not being the easiest as her life was filled with many moments of tragedy and sadness. She did not allow these moments within some difficult pages to define her story. As so many women of Christ strive to achieve the calling of Proverbs 31, my grandmother's life was the walking definition of those verses. God used her to beautifully script the love of Him upon every page within her journey—teaching and leading everyone within her pages. She left a legacy of Christ scripted in permanent ink across the lives of her children, grandchildren, and great-grandchildren. Thinking of the promise of Psalm 30:5, we celebrate that she has found her ultimate JOY and reward in heaven.

As I walk closer to finding that eternal JOY, I will live a life striving to reflect Him. A life resembling the beautiful example provided by the inspiring chapters of my grandmother's life. A life lived in full recognition of His JOY, and a life now rejoicing within the eternal joy of heaven.

I don't know if Carlyle's visions of my grandmother were real, but I do know the authenticity of hope and joy that they provided. One thing I do know for certain is the radiance and joy-filled beauty described within my daughter's dreams only pale in comparison to the beauty that my grandmother radiates within her eternity. An image that I am reminded of often, upon every glimpse within the flutter of beautiful butterfly wings. This radiance, something that I will look forward to with the passing of each page. As MercyMe so beautifully exclaims, "I Can Only Imagine!"

As I long to experience the ultimate joy found within an eternity with our Savior, I am reminded of the all-consuming calling upon our life. A calling that is filled with the joy-filled experiences of heaven on earth. As mentioned in chapter one, I truly believe that He desires for us to live our very best life now with genuine real JOY beginning the moment we accept Him as our personal Lord and Savior. His beautifully scripted plans for His children, while on this journey toward heaven, are also far greater than we can imagine. We all have been called and instructed to not only live a life full of His abundant joy and undeserving grace but charged with the important task of sharing this incredible news throughout our journey toward heaven. A journey that is overflowing with real genuine awe-inspiring joy—joy that is written upon each word of every chapter within His presence. This joy is already scripted upon each page of our journey but becomes one's own choice to discover and recognize that great joy found within each turn of the page.

Chapter 13

RECOGNITION OF GENUINE JOY

As I try to imagine the unimaginable within Heaven, I am excited about the joy that defines my eternity; but I am also incredibly encouraged by the recognition of the genuine joy intertwined within each moment of my every day. God truly has sculpted such beautiful moving joy throughout each chapter and within every moment, but it is up to each one of us to realize and recognize that joy. A joy that resembles the beautiful moving color of the wings within my daughter's dreams, this is a joy that can not be adequately described with words. Words are not descriptive enough to define the beauty found within the genuine joy that He has placed within each of our moments. I am convinced that we are called to seek, see, and enjoy the everyday blessing of this indescribable joy. He has created and called each of His children to live a life that radiates His love and beauty; this life becoming a reality once one realizes and recognizes the importance of living with a full recognition of the joy that envelops each moment.

I am overwhelmed as I begin to truly see the undeserving beauty within the joy of my every day! As my heart begins to try and interpret the abundance of joy found within His plan, it is sometimes more than can be comprehended. The realization and recognition of the significance found within the simplicity of each chapter is sometimes more than I can handle. God does not want us to miss even one fiber of joy that fills our every breath. Often one searches for the grandiose within life to provide the happiness that our souls desire. I have discovered, realized, and recognized that this happiness is truly temporary and always fleeting, but the genuine joy produced through a life lived within His calling is lasting and truly satisfies the soul. I praise him within this recognition just as it is exclaimed in the praise to God for our living Hope found in the following verses:

"Praise be to the God and Father of our Lord
Jesus Christ! In his great mercy he has given

us new birth into a living hope through the resurrection of Jesus Christ from the dead, and into an inheritance that can never perish, spoil, or fade. This inheritance is kept in heaven for you, who through faith are shielded by God's power until the coming of the salvation that is ready to be revealed in the last time. In all this you greatly rejoice, though now for a little while you may have had to suffer grief in all kind of trials. These have come so that the proven genuineness of your faith—of greater worth than gold, which perishes even though refined by fire—may result in praise, glory and honor when Jesus Christ is revealed. Though you have not seen him, you love him; and even though you do not see him now, you believe in him and are filled with an inexpressible and glorious JOY, for you are receiving the end result of your faith, the salvation of your souls." (1 Peter 1: 3–9)

As children of the one true King, we are truly filled with an inexpressible and glorious JOY. A joy that starts the moment of salvation, and a joy that is intertwined within every fiber of our existence. A joy that our Heavenly Father has lavished upon our life, and calls us to recognize now within our journey toward an inheritance in heaven. I can only imagine, as mentioned, the inheritance of our eternity with Him, and the day that I will see Him face to face; but I fully recognize the underserving joy that He has placed within my journey toward that day. I am reminded within this recognition how often we miss the simple blessings of joy that are so intertwined within our every day life. These moments being simple and small, but perfectly scripted and impactful within their purpose. I am so incredibly thankful for the recognition of this undeserving blessing that is scripted upon every page of my life.

One normal day on a quiet drive through rural Mississippi, God flooded my heart with the reminder of this immeasurable JOY that comes only from Him. Within the stillness of my car, He reminded me of the simple beauty found within my every-day life, and the joy found within that beauty. These simple moments not defined by any means of grandiose or excitement, but moments recognized as pure heart exploding joy.

I have realized and recognized the genuine joy found within the simple blessings of my life. I am thankful as God continues to use each of these beautiful blessings to fill the pages of my every chapter and to produce lasting joy. I am overwhelmed by His joy found within my husbands smile, my kid's laughter, my mother's voice, my dad's work ethic, my sister's sweet spirit, my brother's heart, my sister in law's humor, my grandmother's handwriting, my cousin connections, my Inna's selfless service, my brother in law's wit, my friend's text, my church's vision, and ultimately my Savior's love.

Joy, as stated, is mentioned throughout God's word. One discovers their one true source of this joy upon salvation, but it becomes one's choice to realize and recognize the blessing of this joy scripted throughout each chapter of one's life. I have realized and recognized the JOY found within my salvation, and the blessings of joy that this relationship produces throughout each chapter of my life. A life characterized as a journey filled with immeasurable blessings, pages of heartache and pain, chapters of triumph and failure, underserving grace and mercy, beautiful love and redemption, and a victorious ending of eternal joy.

> "May the God of hope fill you with all joy and peace as you trust in him, so that you may overflow with hope by the power of the Holy Spirit." (Romans 15:13)

About the Author

Photographed by
Amy Reeves Halstead

Missy Carruth is a child of God, a wife, a mother, a daughter, a sister, and a friend. She is a first time author who lives with her husband and three children in the same small town where she was raised. Her life's purpose is defined within her relationship with Christ as she strives to live a life that points others toward Him. As a saved child of God, she has recognized within each chapter of life that there is incredible joy, and within that joy is a calling of great responsibility. Missy has accumulated multiple titles and awards throughout her life, but she has recognized that her genuine joy comes only from her true identity in Christ. She is living her most joy-filled life in small-town Mississippi surrounded by her family. Guided by Christ, Missy juggles the joy and adventure of being a wife and working mother.

CPSIA information can be obtained
at www.ICGtesting.com
Printed in the USA
BVHW071522090919
557952BV00001B/229/P